# The Cat in the Window

# The Cat in the Window

## And Other Stories of the Cats We Love

Callie Smith Grant

**Revell**

a division of Baker Publishing Group
Grand Rapids, Michigan

Published by Revell
a division of Baker Publishing Group
P.O. Box 6287, Grant Rapids, Michigan 49516-6287
www.revellbooks.com

Printed in the United States of America

Library of Congress Cataloging-in-Publication Data
Grant, Callie Smith.
    The cat in the window : and other stories of the cats we love / Callie Smith Grant.
        pages cm
    Summary: "A heartwarming collection of true stories about the connections between humans and their cats"— Provided by publisher.
    ISBN 978-0-8007-2180-0 (pbk. : alkaline paper)
    1. Cats—Anecdotes. 2. Cat owners—Anecdotes. 3. Human-animal relationships—Anecdotes. I. Title.
SF445.5.G73 2013
636.8—dc23                                                      2013023243

16   17   18   19        7   6

This book is dedicated to my wonderful in-laws,
Joan and Jack, who truly treat me like a daughter.
Thanks so much for your love and support.

And it is dedicated to all the heroes
at humane societies, shelters,
and rescue organizations
whose ultimate goal is a world
in which such places
are no longer needed.

# Contents

7

# Contents

# Contents

# Introduction

*Callie Smith Grant*

Let's put to rest the silly competition between cats and dogs—or rather, between cat people and dog people.

I realize that many people consider themselves either a cat person or a dog person (I'm not one to choose sides; I'm a fan of both). But let's agree that cats and dogs are unique creations, made so differently they really should not be compared to each other at all. That said, here's an interesting fact: American homes have far more cats than dogs. Not that we're competing, of course!

I am one lucky person in that I get to curl up and read story after story about this very cool beast, the cat—and then pass the really good stories on to you, the reader. As you read on, you'll find cat stories as varied as the fur patterns on cats—some charming, some serious, and everything in between. You'll meet cats who show up at what seems to be an appointed time—not just for the cat, but also for the human in some kind of need. You'll read stories about cats finding just the right home and humans finding just the right cat. There are stories from moms whose interactions with cats help them and their families in surprising ways. One cat lives happily in a fourth-grade classroom and becomes a teacher of sorts himself. I'm always excited to find a story where a cat directly saved a life, and that's here, too. Sometimes a cat shows up mysteriously, sometimes it's not so mysterious—just blessed—but often it seems that the Creator of the beasts of the earth directed a cat's padded feet straight to where the cat needed to go.

It is always my hope that these stories will not only be an entertaining read for you, but might also prompt you to adopt another deserving cat if you can. I know the many writers in this book who went to their local shelters to find their special companion will be inspiring to you. You'll even meet one writer who rescues and fosters kittens and cats—an amazing 1,200 of them so far!

This is a book filled with felines wherever they may be and however they came about. In these pages are indoor cats, outdoor cats, pampered cats, working cats, stray cats, litters of cats—cats who live in houses, on porches, in barns, in laps, or wherever else they may land. But let's still encourage cat people to spay and neuter and to consider keeping a beloved cat indoors. Let me take a minute to remind us all of the following three facts: Too many unwanted kittens are born every day, a cat has a better quality of life when it's been spayed or neutered, and most cats live better and longer lives if they live indoors.

Now, before you curl up in your chair and read on, let me share one more thing about the dog-and-cat competition. I know I started out saying we should put it to rest, but before we do that, let's have a chuckle. My first two animal-themed anthologies included a book of cat stories and a book of dog stories that were published at the same time at Baker Publishing Group. It became kind of fun at the publishing house to track how the two books sold side by side. This tracking, of course, has a whiff of that competition between those calling themselves dog people or cat people.

So which book sold better? The dog book. At first. Then sales of the cat book not only caught up with the dog book, they actually took over.

Steve Oates is a marketing man at Baker—and a man who keeps a photo of his cat on his cell phone and grows his own catnip. I've received many fun emails regarding the feline world from Steve over time, but here's my favorite. He copied me on an email he wrote to Dwight Baker, president of Baker Publishing Group and an animal lover himself, regarding the ongoing sales of my first two books, and it went like this:

> Please correct me if I'm not reading the numbers correctly, but it appears that the sales of these books are pretty much just like cats and dogs themselves. The dog wagged his tail and was eager to get started, but the cat, with a slower and steadier approach, has now handily surpassed the dog in usefulness.

Dwight replied:

> If these books behave in the retail stores in the manner of their subjects, the dog book leaps on incoming customers, barking and slobbering. The cat book will sit apart from the entire scene, waiting patiently for the approach of a customer who is worthy of consideration. Most people will fail to reach acceptable standards as a book buyer, regardless of their income or intent.

Are cat people surprised?

I hope you have as nice a time reading these stories as I did pulling them together. And may God bless you and your pet—or in your endeavors to pair up with the perfect one.

---

### A Wise Man Said It

"There are two means of refuge from the misery of life: music and cats."

—Albert Schweitzer

---

# The Cat in the Window

## Callie Smith Grant

Suffice it to say that a lot of unfortunate factors conspired together in the case of Percy the cat. The details aren't necessary to this story, really, because in the end, they simply added up to one thing: Percy needed to pack up his pet carrier and move to a new home.

That's where I came in. Percy's human was an old friend of mine who was in the middle of some hard life events. For weeks I had been asking my friend what I could do to help. "Nothing," she told me, "but thanks for asking." Then one day she said with some hesitation, "Well, there is something . . . can you find Percy a new home?"

It is not easy to re-home any cat, much less a nine-year-old cat who sheds big time and yowls a lot, so I knew what I was in for. I couldn't take Percy myself, since I already live with two aging cats—and I knew I couldn't throw a new cat into that mix. But I nevertheless immediately promised my stressed friend I would find Percy a home—and if not, I would take him to my local Humane Society, which I knew would not euthanize a cat simply because he's hard to place.

"Send me a picture of him to show people," I told my friend, and soon a photo arrived. Percy was a white long-haired male with gold eyes. He was half Maine coon, so he was a big, handsome guy, except for a wilted ear from a previous ear infection. But the picture I received did not exactly showcase Percy's positive features. It was a head shot of the cat from the neck up, glaring directly at the camera with his eyes half closed and that one ear crumpled down. This wasn't a photo; it was a mug shot. All it needed was a prisoner ID number across the bottom.

And yet people responded to that picture very positively. The wilted ear definitely got the "Awww . . ." response from anyone who saw it. My friends at the Humane Society liked the picture too and were very positive about Percy's prospects. They assured me that I most likely would find him a home, and if not, they would. "White cats are easier to place," they told me, "especially ones with the Maine coon lineage." That took the pressure off, but I knew it was preferable to find Percy a home, not a cage.

Here was the odd thing: I didn't actually know Percy. Even though he had been with my friend for his entire life, I never saw him. I love cats, but this cat always hid when I visited. In Percy's entire nine years, I'd only seen a streak of white at his home. In order to find him the right home, I felt I needed somehow to know him.

During my next visit to Percy's home, I asked to see him and was shown to the bedroom where Percy was perched on the only windowsill in the small apartment. He liked it there, watching birds in good weather or leaning against the window in winter sun. I spoke his name. He took one look at me and quickly left his window perch to slink under the bed. That was the end of that. The next visit a couple weeks later, the same thing happened—Percy slept in the window until I entered the room and spoke to him. Down he went and under the bed, not to be seen for the rest of my visit.

I was feeling some concern about this. I lived a hundred miles away and could only put so much time into this getting-to-know-you activity and still hold down a job. But, as the cliché goes, three times a charm, and indeed the third visit proved to be fruitful. This time I found Percy not in the window but on top of the queen-sized bed, curled up on a corner. I stood in the doorway of the bedroom, and he looked up at me with half-opened eyes.

I once knew a self-described Crazy Cat Lady who insisted that you should always tell a cat what you're about to do before you act. So I did. I stayed in the doorway and spoke gently. "Percy, you need to let me know you so I can find you a new home."

Percy watched me, but this time he stayed put. I moved to the bed and perched on the opposite corner. He remained where he was, watching. I slowly stretched out on my side to lower myself to his level. He watched me, and he stayed.

Now I remembered a cat behaviorist on TV saying that when approaching a strange cat, take off your eyeglasses if you wear them and extend the stems to the cat so it can sniff "who" you are.

Well, why not? I took off my glasses and extended the stems across the bed to Percy. He immediately leaned forward and sniffed with great interest the right stem, then the left one, then the right one again, then the left one again. Then he shocked me by flopping onto his side and showing me his belly.

What to do? First I talked to him. "Oh, Percy," I cooed, "you are a handsome boy." Then I reached out and scratched under his chin, his cheeks, his forehead, keeping all action above the neck. He stretched and purred and flexed his big toes in obvious feline bliss. I continued to say glowing things to him while he preened: "What a gorgeous guy you are, Percy. My goodness. You are one magnificent creature. Anyone would like to have you."

For nearly five minutes I praised Percy while he stretched and purred and flexed his hammy feet. Then he fixed his golden eyes on mine and looked suddenly startled. I imagined him thinking, *What am I DOING?* He hurled himself off the bed and under it.

But that was enough for me to feel complete confidence that I could represent Percy honestly and positively to someone who might want him. In fact, had I not had my aging lady-cats at home, I would have taken him myself. I drove home encouraged.

Back home I talked about Percy to a couple I knew, and they were interested at first. Then the husband finally shook his head. "No, I really don't want a long-haired cat," he said. I chose not to be discouraged. The good news is that they got so interested in acquiring a cat that they went to the county animal shelter and picked out a delightful short-haired cat for themselves—one that otherwise may never have been adopted. So because Percy needed a good home, another cat got a good one.

I had to go on an out-of-state trip before I found Percy a home. The day before the trip, my cat-sitter friend, Mary Ann, was sitting at my table chatting. I talked to her about Percy's mug shot and showed it to her just for giggles. Mary Ann looked at it for a minute and said, "I want that cat."

I was surprised. "You do?"

"Yes."

"Are you sure?"

"I'm sure."

"Do you want to think about it?"

"No, I don't need to think about it. I want that cat."

This possibility had not occurred to me because Mary Ann's previous living situation hadn't allowed her to have pets. But she had recently bought her own house, so this was very fortunate timing. I began to make plans to pick up Percy and transport him a hundred miles from the only home he'd ever known to move in with Mary Ann. And for a variety of reasons, I was the one who would need to do it. I emailed many cat-lover friends and asked for their prayers and for any advice to help Percy and me pull this off without too much misery.

The big day came, and I drove the hundred miles north to my friend's place. That day, for the first time, Percy showed himself to me voluntarily. Apparently he knew my voice and my scent now, because he sashayed into the living room where I sat, stuck his tail straight up, yowled at me, and rubbed on me. This was the first time I'd ever seen Percy up and walking, and what a gorgeous cat. He had that big lion's chest of a Maine coon and a full, stunning coat. He was over sixteen pounds, and yet he was a lean sixteen pounds—a whole lot of Percy was fur. He rubbed and rubbed on me, back and forth, and I scratched him all over his big handsome body. Then he took himself back to his window.

Hours later, my friend and I silently agreed that the time had come. We grabbed Percy and his carrier—a nice roomy dog carrier, fortunately—and did the deed. He clawed at me going in and drew some blood, but we got him in. Then the yowling began. I draped the carrier with towels that smelled like his home, tucked him onto the bucket seat next to me in the car, waved good-bye to my friend, and headed out. It was raining as I drove Percy to the interstate. I talked to him until we got on the highway, but he had ceased his vocalizing. So I stopped talking. I'd had fears of frightened yowling for the next two hours, but he never made a peep the entire trip. Halfway there, I saw that he'd dozed off.

At our destination, I lugged Percy through the rain to the front door of Mary Ann's tidy little cottage and into her open, eager arms. This house was completely cat-ready—toys, treats, brush, places to perch, you name it. Of course, we should have left Percy crated for his own cat-insecurity reasons for a while, but Mary Ann and I simply got too excited. We opened the carrier door. Ta-da! Of course, Percy immediately shot under the bed.

Mary Ann and I took that time to go over the house. Everything was spot-on ready for the big guy, and I was particularly pleased to count ten windows Percy could enjoy. I left after a while, and I learned that Percy ventured out about ten minutes later. He examined every room in the house, and then he cozied up to Mary Ann, who brushed and brushed him. They fell in love.

It wasn't easy to merge their lives at first. We really should have gradually introduced Percy to the new home, and I've since learned that a lot of his yowling and acting out for the next two weeks was his way of trying to find his place in his new world. It took some time for him to feel comfortable with the windows, too. I was thinking like a human, of course—going from one window on the fourth floor of a city apartment to ten windows on the ground floor in the country sounded to me like the Big Time for a cat. It was that, but it was also unnerving and unsettling for Percy. It took a couple weeks of all-night yowling with the patient Mary Ann using ear protection before Percy finally turned a corner, settled in, and settled down.

Now the big white cat enjoys all the windows of his home. When Mary Ann mows the lawn, he moves from open window to open window to watch her work and to breathe in the fragrances of the outdoors. He watches wild life moving about in the yard. He runs around the house in the full moon at night, window to window. He talks to his new human, who adores him and brushes him, and he follows her around the house like the cool companion he is. They're still in love.

In the end, I'm pleased to tally up that, because of Percy, not far from my house live two other happy cats and their three happy owners. And I feel pretty good myself.

*a full moon tonight*
*cat in window cannot sleep*
*neither can humans*

# Miss Scarlett and Rhett

*Vicki Crumpton*

This is a tale of two kitties.

For seventeen years I was owned by Miss Scarlett, a striking black cat with perhaps the most presence of any feline I've known. When she spent a few days in Atlanta getting radioactive iodine treatment for a thyroid problem, even the staff at the clinic said, "She's got presence!"

But as these things happen, Miss S came to the end of her days. She left a hole in our hearts and in that of her daughter, a reclusive calico named Patches. We wondered how Patches would fare without her constant companion.

One toasty July day about two weeks later, my husband, Ed, came in from work about lunchtime. He's an electrical engineer, and his work often takes him to a large industrial facility about twelve miles from our home. Because of the nature of their work, the facility is a secure area surrounded by barbed-wire fences and set well away from houses and roads, which made it rather unusual that Ed got to his big Dodge diesel truck and found a small gray-and-white kitty in the parking lot. Checking to make sure the kitty wasn't going to run under his truck, Ed climbed into the cab and drove home, averaging a speed of 55 mph. When he arrived, he mentioned the kitty to me, and the oddity of it being at his jobsite. Later that night we drove the truck to a local barbecue place a few miles away.

Now, I know that astute readers are already well ahead of me here, but after we ordered our meal, one of the servers came to us and asked, "Is that your big red truck in the parking lot?" We looked at each other and nodded. "There's a kitten . . ." the server said. We got up and found the owner of the barbecue place holding the cutest little kitten with about the biggest kitten ears we'd ever seen. "Is this yours?" he asked. We told him that despite Ed's efforts, this little guy must have somehow climbed underneath that big truck and found a secure enough spot to survive a ride home and to lunch. "That's okay," the owner said, "I'll just put him in the back with all the others. People know I feed scraps to strays, so they're always dropping cats here."

You could say that Ed and I have a soft spot for animals. Okay, I'll just say it flat out: "My name is Vicki and I love animals." There, my secret is out.

We looked at each other and knew that we couldn't leave Big Ears to his own devices. He came home with us, but this time in the cab of the truck.

Ed called the PR office at the plant, and they posted an announcement about the kitten. When no one called us to claim the little guy, we knew he'd become part of our family. We just wondered how he'd get along with Patches. But you could say that he threw himself at her until she gave in. He even persuaded her to enjoy wrestling with him a bit, which is no small feat considering that she really does not like other cats.

What would we call him? I don't remember any of the names we tried on, although I'm sure there were a few. Then one day it dawned on me that we could honor Miss Scarlett by giving the kitty a name reflective of Miss Scarlett's heritage.

Patches and her mom had been strays in my neighborhood in Nashville. One day I decided to put out some food for a thin black cat and her baby. It took a lot of patience and coaxing, but eventually both mama and kitty became mine. And when mama cat got access to good food on a regular schedule, her, uh, appreciation of it became immediately obvious. I named her after the character in *Gone with the Wind* who famously said, "As God as my witness, I'll never be hungry again."

In honor of Miss Scarlett, little kitty with the big ears would be Rhett.

Since then, Patches and Rhett have both needed respective life-saving treatments. Patches received her own radioactive iodine treatment. Rhett required a complete urinary reconstruction and had to endure both a Brazilian bikini wax and an Elizabethan collar. He did that with his usual style and flair. We joke about him having good taste in trucks because not every truck in that parking lot would have sprung for two trips to the city and a specialist to do his surgery.

We share our lives with quite a few animals, and one thing amazes me about them. They can teach us the hardest lessons by example, and often without any sighing or whining on their parts. That's certainly not always my approach when life dishes out an unexpected or unwelcome turn. Somehow animals seem to understand that the things we do "to" them—whether radioactive iodine injections or an embarrassing shave in the south forty, as we might say in Texas—are really done out of love and in their best interest in the long run. Animals somehow seem to rise above it all and make the best of every day and every situation.

# The Time-Share Cat

## *Andrea Doering*

About two minutes after my husband, Ron, and I moved our family into our first house, the pleas for a pet began. Now that we were out of an apartment, with a property of our own, our three children knew what we needed—a pet. I hated being the voice of reason, but I kept firm to my opinion that it just wasn't fair to leave a pet alone all day long. "Pets are social—we can't get a pet right now." With both Ron and me commuting two hours a day, I didn't see how we could manage to add the care of another being.

I remember thinking that a move to the suburbs would be a good thing—a slower pace, a bit more fresh air, some quiet. We moved to a town with shady streets and a real sense of small-town life. But even as we enjoyed the changes our move brought, life felt full of hard edges and nonnegotiables. Between train schedules, daycare drop-off and pick-up schedules, and parking and town regulations to navigate, our days felt pressed and squeezed. We'd barely had time to meet any neighbors, and most did not have children the same age as our own.

I was extracting Emily, our oldest at four years old, from her car seat one afternoon, and instead of scrambling out to join her siblings, she looked at me and said, "Mom, I just don't think I can stand it if we never have a pet."

Emily is known for the dramatic, and if not for her tone of voice, I might have tossed this remark off as another theatrical moment. But it was a soft whisper of a thought, and that softness sifted past and through all the hard edges of the day and just about broke my heart. As we walked into the house I sent up a silent prayer—well, maybe an ultimatum—to God. "This one's up to you. I don't see how this can happen, but you do."

A few weeks later God apparently had the answer. Emily opened the back door one morning and I heard a soft "Ooohh" escape her mouth. There on the back porch sat an orange tiger-striped cat, as if he'd patiently been waiting for her to show up.

Well, much activity ensued. While Ron and I breakfasted that Saturday, Emily roused her younger siblings. Then came a heated discussion of how much milk they should give the cat. This was all taking place in the house, as the cat, whom I forbade entry, sat waiting on the porch. And he did seem to be waiting. When presented with a bowl of milk, he happily obliged by drinking it and allowed his benefactors the chance to pet him for a few minutes before he scampered off down the street.

All day long the cat was the topic of discussion. Where had he come from? Would he come back? What would they feed him when he did? What should they name him? Of course he needed a name. The scenarios seemed endless, and I remember that day thinking how easily everyone got along. I had no idea if the cat would come back, but I was grateful for that day, and thankful God had heard a young girl's desire.

But God apparently was not finished. The cat, by this time named Tiger, returned again and again. Each time in the morning, each time ready for a meal and some attention. By the third or fourth day I thought perhaps we'd better see if he was lost. He had a collar and there was a number on it. I was the only one who thought we should call. The real possibility that our part-time cat would disappear was untenable to the children.

Finally, the next afternoon we mustered up the courage to call, me on the phone with the owner with three heads at my elbow. When I hung up, I smiled. "Would you like to go see your cat and meet her owner?" Though Ron had been an amused onlooker to the cat saga, even he was intrigued, and all five of us trekked across the street and one level up. On the top floor of a butter-yellow Victorian house was an apartment. The owner waited at the top of the steps to welcome us, and as the children rounded the corner, they saw their friend stretched out on a window seat in the sunshine. His name was Sammy, and his owner was a generous, happy woman who laughed a lot and seemed to enjoy the company of children.

We learned that Sammy had many stops in his day. One neighbor saw him around noon, another in the late afternoon, another in the evening. The previous owner of our house had been the morning stop. He was a man with cerebral palsy whose days were definitely brightened by Sammy, but the man had been gone over a year by the time we purchased the house, and Sammy's owner was surprised to find Sammy had "put us in the rotation" as it were. "He gets plenty to eat here and other places, so don't feel like you have to feed him," she told me. "But he loves to visit people, and everyone seems to love him back. You kids are welcome to come see him anytime he's at home, too."

We walked home for lunch. Nothing had changed, and yet everything had. We had a pet. A part-time one, but that was what we *could* have, and that was what God provided. We had met a neighbor and learned a bit about our other neighbors—they were cat people, and they liked to share. The world seemed softer somehow with a cat in our lives, and as I looked up the street where three lively children were bouncing along, deep in conversation, I could see that our new house was on the way to becoming a home.

### Is Your Cat a Southpaw?

Pets can have a paw preference. Maybe you already observed that. It's certainly not unusual for your cat to use the same paw consistently to do things cats do. But now researchers think many animals do have preference for left or right. For this we needed a study? Well, actually the studies are to inform future breeding and behaviors, but the information they provide can be fun stuff. For example, researchers discovered that when your cat wants something, she'll reach for it with her dominant paw. But if she's playing, she'll use either paw or both paws.[1]

# Fat Jimmy from Jersey

### Alison Hodgson

We were going to the airport to pick up a cat, which was the first I heard about Fat Jimmy. But he wasn't going to be our cat, my mother was quick to add. Fat Jimmy belonged to my aunt who lived in New Jersey. She was moving to an apartment that didn't allow animals. We lived in Michigan and Fat Jimmy was flying into Detroit. My aunt in Indiana was going to take custody, and we were doing her a favor fetching the cat from the airport and delivering him.

At the airport, my mother told the baggage attendant we were there about a cat.

"Oh, yes!" He hustled off and disappeared behind swinging doors.

We heard Fat Jimmy before we saw him. A loud and plaintive meowing came from a distance, gaining volume, until the doors swung open and a dog crate was wheeled up to us. I shouldn't have been surprised. I already knew Fat Jimmy was an unfathomable twenty-two pounds; his mother had nearly died giving birth and needed a C-section. Even so, peering through the slits, I was astonished to see the biggest cat outside the pages of the *Guinness World Records*: Fat Jimmy indeed.

My dad hoisted the kennel, and Fat Jimmy began to meow louder and even more plaintively. The baggage attendant watched us walk away. "There goes another satisfied passenger," he said.

The plan was to take Fat Jimmy to our house for the night so he could recuperate after his long flight. We would drive down to Indiana the next day. The entire way home, Jimmy did not stop bellowing. By the time we got to our house he was hoarse.

Dad carried the crate into our dining room and opened it without hesitation. A giant orange cannonball shot out and lodged itself under the china cabinet. I don't know how. This same cabinet is in my daughter's room today, used as a bookcase. For the sake of veracity, I measured the space between the floor and the bottom of the cabinet, a mere three inches. I saw that enormous cat wedged underneath it with my own eyes, and I can't believe it happened.

The laws of physics might bend, but they will not break. The cabinet tipped and would have fallen forward, but my father held it with one hand and, with the other, pulled the cat out and hurled him across the room. Fat Jimmy landed on all four paws and streaked under the sofa, where he stayed the rest of the night and had to be dragged out the next morning. I'm sure my parents were relieved to surrender him to my Indiana aunt and uncle later that day.

Fat Jimmy didn't last a week.

"He was a coward and a bully," my aunt from New Jersey now freely admits. I don't know if she thought to warn her sister when she was trying to pawn him off. Perhaps she did and then thought again.

We certainly saw his cowardice in Michigan, but he didn't have time or an appropriate victim to bully. In Indiana he spent a day or two hidden under their sofa, but within minutes of summoning the strength to venture out, he found my aunt and uncle's sweet old cat, Fern, and gave her a trouncing, nearly killing her.

"We can't keep this cat," my Indiana uncle told my New Jersey aunt, who called my mom in Michigan and begged her to take in Fat Jimmy.

I know my father was reluctant, and I can only imagine the discussions my parents had behind closed doors. We didn't have the official motto "You do for family," but we did, regardless. Fat Jimmy was going to be our cat—only temporarily, my father was quick to tell us.

Despite having picked him up from the airport, hosting him for a night, and driving him to Indiana, none of us had seen more than a glimpse of the cat. When he returned to us, we released him in the living room and he shot under the sofa. He cowered there for an appropriate amount of time until he gathered the strength to creep out and explore his new home.

Twenty-two pounds is a lot of cat, but in spite of his name, Fat Jimmy wasn't really as fat as you might think. He was a big cat, certainly, but his big head and massive frame contributed significantly. His mother was a tiny little Manx named Rabbit, who had no tail at all. Fat Jimmy's father was a giant cat. Fat Jimmy, being only half Manx, had a short, rigid tail, about four inches long. When he was excited it vibrated rather than swayed. He was bright orange with touches of white. You wouldn't call him handsome exactly, but Fat Jimmy was a cat to be proud of.

And his name fit him to a T. Regrettably, one of my brother's friends, Jim, who also answered to Jimmy and was a little soft around the belly, thought we had named the cat for him. I was appalled when he admitted this twenty-five years after the fact.

"That was his *name*!" I said. "He came to us that way!"

Fortunately this perceived insult didn't prevent Jim from marrying one of my Wisconsin cousins twenty years later.

"How *did* he get the name Fat Jimmy?" I asked my New Jersey aunt.

"He was such a brilliant shade of orange. I don't know what ridiculous, inappropriate name I wanted to call him . . . Marmalade? I can't remember, but your Uncle Gil said, 'That's not any name for a cat like that!' And he named him Fat Jimmy."

Well-played, Uncle Gil, well-played.

Once he found the strength to come out from under our sofa, Fat Jimmy made himself at home and sauntered around like he owned the place, until he got scared, which happened frequently. Jimmy's fear response was the traditional fight or flight, the latter being his preference, but it was his execution of flight that set him apart. His natural instinct was to climb, but his girth prevented him from getting far. Terror and strength combined to help him hold on, and it was common to see Fat Jimmy hanging halfway up a tree like a giant orange growth.

He wasn't ornamental in the traditional sense, and he was no hunter, but there was just something about Fat Jimmy. My sister, Torey, adored him, and he was fairly tolerant of her. She liked to dress him up and he would allow it, to a point. When he was over having a diaper from Torey's Cabbage Patch doll jammed on his rear, he would signal his dismay with a low moan. It took Torey a few times to understand that whenever she played with Jimmy, an internal timer was set, and the low-pitched humming was the timer going off. If she didn't release him before he ended the hum, he lifted his big paw, extended his claws, and clobbered her, usually on the face.

So he wasn't a looker or helpful or consistently good with children, but we all loved him, even my dad. We probably would have kept him forever and ever except he started to urinate in the shower of an infrequently used bathroom. It was disgusting but manageable.

Unfortunately he branched out. More regrettably, his next choice was my parents' large walk-in closet, specifically my father's garment bag, which was stored in the corner. No one knows how many times Fat Jimmy crept into that dark spot and did his wet and private business. We do know the garment bag was waterproof and acted like a basin for the pooling moisture, and one day my father grabbed it, in his fast and forceful way, and Fat Jimmy's urine splashed all over his arms, his shirt, and his face.

And that was that.

"Fat Jimmy has to go," Dad told my mother who informed my New Jersey aunt, who had long before bought a house and acquired another cat.

Fat Jimmy was shipped back to her and my New Jersey uncle and—by then—cousins, and lived quite happily another decade. He did not stop his inappropriate urinating *and* he lived a good life. They loved Jimmy, and every night he slept with his head on my cousin's pillow after my aunt sang a lullaby—to the cat. Any way you calculate it, Fat Jimmy lived a good, long life, and died, as the Bible says, "old and full of years."

Mom recently said, "Your dad loved Fat Jimmy. I think if it hadn't hit his face, Fat Jimmy would have gotten by . . . maybe."

## A Little Humor for Little Humans

Q: What does a cat say when it's surprised?
A: Me-WOW!

Q: What's the difference between a cat and a frog?
A: A cat has nine lives but a frog croaks every day.

Q: Why did the cat have trouble using its computer?
A: Because it kept eating the mouse.

Q: What is a cat's favorite dessert?
A: Mice cream.

Q: What did one cat say to another?
A: Can you hear me meow?[2]

# The Gift of St. Nicholas

## Kathryn Ann Mays

It had been an unusually snowy and windy first week of December. The temperatures had plummeted to the teens most days. But the snow was a welcome sight to our family. We always looked forward to snow on St. Nicholas Eve, December 5. We had been celebrating this festival, which originated in Europe, in our home since our five children were small. This is the night that St. Nicholas brings a bag of gifts and goodies and leaves them on the doorstep. He knocks on the door, and by the time the children run to open it, he has disappeared. Not once had our children been able to catch a glimpse of "the old man." My husband, Jonathan, and I had arranged different ways to do this bag drop-off during the two decades we had been playing St. Nicholas. This year we left a bag of Christmas goodies and modest gifts in our car and arranged for a friend to come at 8:00 p.m., get the bag out of the car, and put it on our darkened porch, then ring the bell and run.

A few weeks earlier Jonathan and I had discussed what to put in the St. Nicholas bag. Finances were tight that year. Jonathan was only able to find part-time work, and I had some serious health issues then that kept me from working at all. Our two youngest children, ages fourteen and sixteen, were still home, so I suggested we give them a kitten to round out what little we were giving the kids that year. We had a dog and a cat for most of our older children's growing up, but it had been a couple of years since we had had any pets.

But Jonathan said no. He was the one who went through the painful process of being with our cat of fourteen years when she was put down, and he said he didn't want to go through that again. No way to any more pets. I wasn't really happy about it, but I respected his feelings on the matter and dropped the subject.

So on that wintry, blustery December night, we watched the clock as it neared 8:00. We had finished a wonderful dinner with our two youngest children and our daughter's boyfriend. Now we listened to Christmas music and played games together. It was five minutes before eight, and in spite of the howling wind and the music, I heard a faint meow outdoors. I looked at Jonathan. He was looking at me. Really, he was glaring at me. We didn't say anything to each other, but I indicated silently that I had nothing to do with this meow. Jonathan rolled his eyes. I widened mine back trying to tell him that I *really* had nothing to do with anything that meowed.

In our three years living in that neighborhood, we had never seen a cat outside, not even a stray. But we could definitely hear one now. The kids had been watching their parents try to "talk" to each other. Now the kids hopped up and ran to the front door yelling, "It's a *real* St. Nicholas present, a *real* one!" They opened the door.

Sure enough, standing in the dark on the stoop, in the cold and blowing snow, was the skinniest little cat I had ever seen. She was black and white with markings that made her resemble a Holstein cow. She looked up at us and meowed. The kids were thrilled as they picked her up and held her. Upon close inspection, we discovered that we could see every rib and feel the vertebrae on her spine. Her green eyes were alert and shining, though, and she was purring up a storm. We could see that she was a very young mom and she had been nursing babies, who were not with her.

"Do not get attached to her," Jonathan announced. "She goes to the pound tomorrow morning." Protests from all of us were flung his way, but he stood his ground. Rebekah, our sixteen-year-old, and her boyfriend pointed out that the cat would need to be taken care of at least until morning. "She'll need food and a litter box for overnight," Rebekah said. So Jonathan let them go to the store to get those items. In the meantime, I went to the basement to find a box and a warm blanket for this skinny cat with the unusual markings.

By the time I came back upstairs, Jonathan and David, our fourteen-year-old, were talking to each other about what they should name the cat. Shocked, I asked what had changed in the ten minutes I was gone.

"Dad called the gas station up on the highway," David

39

said, "and asked if anyone had left a flyer for a missing cat. Their security cameras caught the cat and some kittens being dropped off in the middle of a snowstorm. They said the cat and her kittens had been living by the Dumpster in the back of the gas station almost all week. Some of the employees took the kittens home."

"Why didn't anyone take the mom?" I asked.

"I don't know," Jonathan answered. I observed that the cat had managed to get herself into his lap. "Maybe they couldn't catch her. But after I heard her story, I can't even think of taking her to the pound. She walked a good three blocks from that gas station in this weather." I was glad to see that my husband's bark was worse than his bite tonight.

Rebekah came back with supplies to the happy news that the cat was staying. "What should we call her?" she said.

In the short time the cat had been in our house, we had already called her two different names. Jonathan called her Skinny Minnie—she truly was skinny. Rebekah called her Minnie Moo because she looked like a cow. Minnie was the common denominator, so Minnie is what she became. At first we would mostly call her Skinny Minnie, but she fattened up nicely, so soon enough that wasn't so appropriate. Minnie Moo was the special loving name that would stick. It also would be the name we would call her when she was in trouble for knocking things over on the dresser at three in the morning.

That first night, however, we marveled together at how this cat came from her Dumpster hiding place across a snowy field, past several houses with their front lights on, and onto our dark front steps on the very night the children were expecting gifts at our front door. We marveled at how loud this little thing had to meow to be heard over the wild wind outside and the Christmas music inside. And we marveled at how she seemed to decide we were the people who needed her just as much as she needed us.

As for me, I marveled that night that it was Jonathan's chest where she slept—in our bed, mind you. That first night—on the Eve of St. Nicholas—our little gift purred the cold and the snow and the wind away and came into our home. And then she stayed.

### Do the Math

Seven times more kittens and puppies are born each year than humans in the United States. Logic dictates that with that ratio, there simply cannot be enough successful pet and human unions. That's reason enough to spay and neuter.

But with cats, the news is especially sobering. According to SpayUSA, one non-spayed cat and her mate and all of their offspring, producing two litters of kittens per year—with an average of 2.8 of those kittens surviving each litter—can total the following:

| | |
|---|---|
| 1 year: | 12 kittens |
| 2 years: | 67 kittens |
| 3 years: | 376 kittens |
| 4 years: | 2,107 kittens |
| 5 years: | 11,801 kittens |
| 6 years: | 66,088 kittens |
| 7 years: | 370,092 kittens |
| 8 years: | 2,072,514 kittens |
| 9 years: | 11,606,077 kittens |

Yes, that's over 11 million cats introduced to the world if we don't spay and neuter. Spread the word. Check out SpayUSA.org to see what you can do to help.

# My Cat, Big Boy

*Mark Muhich*

Galveston is the oldest port city in Texas. Karankawa Indians, Spanish conquistadors, French pirates, slave traders, and Civil War admirals have all sailed into its safe harbor. Like old ports everywhere, old buildings seem to surround the Port of Galveston, and for many years I resided in one. An old WWII Quonset hut housed my welding shop, the last structure closest to the railroad tracks leading down into the docks.

Strange, inexplicable events prove more the rule than the exception on an island like Galveston. One learns to expect the unexpected. So it surprised me not in the least when a scrawny kitten pattered into my shop. Nothing unusual there, I suppose, but that black tabby kitten grew into a huge cat. I named him Big Boy. He stayed with me for fifteen years and would even save my life. This is one of his stories.

Though he was a stray, Big Boy was the most affectionate creature. He seemed to walk on his tiptoes, and most often when he saw me, he ran and jumped into my arms. Big Boy liked to wrestle; we enjoyed many a hand-to-paw combat sustained by my thick leather welding gloves.

Big Boy was fearless. Even when puny, at the first sight of my dogs, he scratched their golden retriever noses—once each—and drew blood. He grew into their tussle mate, chewed their floppy ears, and often slept on top of them when the weather turned cold.

Grain spilling from Midwest hopper cars would sprout between the railroad tracks. Flocks of pigeons would feed there. Of course, port rats, the scourge of grain exporters, proliferated—fat ones, fast ones, mean ones. Rats that lots of other cats would not fight feasted there. Rats bigger than Big Boy himself he killed and dragged into my welding bay.

Summer nights in Galveston are steamy, breathless, sweaty respites from the Texas white-hot sun. The Gulf of Mexico washes the island in salty mists. Humidity amplifies sound. You can hear the surf for miles on the right breeze. One such night, I welded late. The animals rested close by but out of harm from the blazing arc weld. Covered in thick clothes, through my welding helmet, I watched and heard the steel edges sizzle and melt into place.

Close to midnight, the buzz from my welding grew louder. A cicada hatch? No. Was the welding machine broken? No. The sound grew worrisome and built in intensity. Had the water pipes burst? Removing my helmet, I searched the corners of the Quonset hut. A ruptured compressor line? The buzzing noise grew urgent. The menace echoed through the metal Quonset shell growing louder still. I traced the threatening hiss.

The sound came from outside, where a fence met the corrugated arched wall below big catalpa trees, beyond the sharp sheen of the street lamp, in the dark corner where dead leaves had wadded up thick and obscure. The sound was coming from this corner. The high pressure piercing hiss emanated only a few feet beyond my gaze.

My eyes adjusted to the dark, damp night. There was Big Boy, his black tabby fur camouflaged against the gray and black somber shadows. What was he doing out here? Why was Big Boy staring motionless? What was he staring at? Why would he not answer me when I called? My eyes acclimated to the dark, deep recesses of the night. I peered into the black corner. There, the nearly invisible, the shocking . . . the coiled diamond-backed pattern of a rattlesnake.

The sight of a thick snake, wound round and round, half-hidden below the dry leaves, whose length it was impossible to estimate, sickened me. I understood instantly. Big Boy had cornered the rattler at the side of my building, ten feet from my front door. This was a powerful snake that was furious that it had been trapped. Trapped by my cat.

The snake's head waved, its mouth was wide, and its eyes shone like deadly diamonds. Big Boy sat perfectly still, poised, within striking distance of the snake, but just distant enough to make a strike risky for the snake. Big Boy and the rattler must have tangled and taken each other's measure before I stumbled on them in the dark. Neither of them was backing down. The snake's rattles roared in my ears, and my cat's silent stalwart courage guarded against the cornered lethal serpent.

Big rattlers are not unknown on Galveston Island. The Spanish called this Snake Island, and the modern-day Galveston Police Department has a snake patrol officer on call twenty-four hours per day to prove it. I phoned 9-1-1 as the snake rattled loudly in the background. An officer arrived and shone a huge beacon onto the snake cornered by Big Boy. Neither had given an inch.

The police officer slowly, calmly, smoothly lowered a nylon noose toward the snake's angry head. It struck and was snared by the snake stick. The snake made two huge loops in the night air and then hung suspended from the officer's outstretched tool. It was longer than either of us was tall.

"Get me a pillowcase," ordered the officer, "and be sure there are no holes in it."

The officer shuffled the snake's length into my pillowcase and deftly freed its head, tying closed the pillowcase. "I'll release it out on the Pelican Island salt flats," promised the officer. "That is a great snake."

I only nodded in agreement as Big Boy glided back into the shop. Big Boy, to my way of thinking, was by far greater still. We remained best friends for years, Big Boy and I. He went blind and died in one afternoon. I cried my eyes out that day, realizing I had lost but been lucky to know such a brave animal.

# I Thought I Would Slow Down

*Ila J. Smith*

I was going to retire—again! I had already retired from one of those very public organizations where one has to be "on" all the time, and now I was retiring from another such organization. I am not a spring chicken, and I was looking forward to lots and lots of downtime, i.e., sleeping in; long, undisturbed hours reading on the porch; watching all my favorites on TV—you get the picture.

Throughout those working years I was the captain of a group called the Just for Lunch Bunch, urging busy women to stop, slow down, and take themselves to lunch on Fridays—to treat themselves to some downtime. The crew, of course, knew about my plans to kick back in retirement, so several who served on the local Humane Society board said, "Aha! She's the perfect candidate to adopt a pet."

I was amenable to a cat since we had some over the years for the kids. I especially remembered our last cat, Camille: a pretty, long-haired black cat with white face markings. You know the kind—quiet and dignified, sometimes friendly, most times expressing attitude—"I will sit on your lap when I feel like it!" A good cat for slowing down.

I finally made it into retirement, party and all, and the adopt-a-cat discussion continued with the Lunch Bunch crowd, even to the point that one of them was going with me to make the choice. *What? They didn't trust me to do it?* This was a big deal. My daughter—"mom" to my two grand-dogs—came home from another city to take me shopping to properly outfit me in anticipation of my new family member.

True to the Lunch Bunch plan, my friend and adopting advocate went with me to select a nice feline to lounge around with me in my retirement. I was thinking something Camille-like, but somehow I left with a little tiger they had named Cindy Lou. I guess what tipped the scales was that when she was brought to the viewing room, she was a bundle of action, wasn't afraid, and knew what toys were for.

At the next Friday Lunch Bunch I walked into a "kitten shower" —a huge basket beautifully presented with treats, every imaginable toy, catnip gizmos, peacock feathers, a gift card to the pet store, a soft blanket, you name it, to welcome Cindy Lou. It has been three years and we still have new things to open from the shower—what a cool thing. Of course there have been many kitty pictures and Cindy Lou stories shared since.

Cindy Lou is a talker! I seldom have to guess what it is she wants—a small table beside my easy chair is her podium. Up she comes into my face and wants a drink, or wants to go out, or wants me to come to the kitchen while she eats. Oh yes, she doesn't like to eat alone. And a drink—oh no, not from a dish on the floor, not on your life—only from the bathroom faucet.

If I try to ignore her, she gets up on her podium, meows at me, and pokes me on my shoulder with her paw until I respond. If I am fed up and just say a strong "no!" she most likely turns around and flops down with her back to me and pouts for a while. The funniest times are the conversations I have with her earnestly watching me with tilted head while I tell her all the reasons I don't need to get up and do her bidding. Even funnier is when she looks me in the eye and shoves my book off the table and onto the floor. I'm in control? You've got to be kidding.

Remember I mentioned sleeping in during my retirement? Here's my daily routine with Cindy Lou. She rises slowly between 4:30 and 5:00 a.m., gives a little chirp or two, jumps down from where we sleep, and checks out the immediate area. Then my wake-up call begins from the podium—and if I don't move fast enough, there could be shoulder pokes involved. Obviously I caved too soon and the pattern is set, so I put food in her dish, brush my teeth, warm up some coffee, give her some treats, leave the porch door ajar, and crawl back in bed for maybe a half hour of peace.

If it is really cold out, I carefully close the porch door just enough so she can still nudge it open to come back in. She's a hardy girl and likes to be on the porch even in freezing weather. Once when it was pretty cold outside, I accidentally closed the door all the way, then I took a nap and was down for the count. More than an hour passed when I suddenly awoke to her call, and when I let her in, she chewed me out all the way to the kitchen. My bad!

Cindy Lou is very social and greets everyone, stranger or no, who comes to the door. By the same token, she follows me everywhere, talking all the time. My office and computer are no exception. She used to fit nicely on top of the monitor when she was a kitten. She still gets up there to supervise my work or fall asleep, but now that she's grown, one leg invariably hangs off. And the printer is a fascinating thing that I have to be stern about because she wants to "help" the paper come through.

Cindy Lou has all the family and many of my friends wrapped around her little paws. My grand-dogs send her emails telling her about their escapades; for the golden retriever, that means sneaking food off the counters, and she gives Cindy Lou tips on how she can do the same. My kitten grew up to be a long-legged and svelte cat even though she eats a lot, and her markings are beautiful, her fur especially soft and fine. Even the delivery guy pets her and remarks about it. If she were human she would definitely win a beauty contest. It is odd how things strike you— once my son-in-law remarked that she had big feet, and I was a little offended. After I thought about it, he's right, she does have big feet—but she's still a beauty.

She loves my lap at every opportunity, whether it is convenient or not—I can only do that crossword or read that book holding it on one side or the other of her lap place. Retirement turned out to be a lot different than I expected—and a lot better from what I expected, all because of a smart, sassy, four-legged, big-footed feline named Cindy Lou.

*window cat rises*
*from her warm nest of blankets*
*watches falling leaves*

# The Long Road Home

## Mary Ann Osborn

In 2005 I moved to Mississippi. I had been caregiver to my beloved grandfather in Michigan for the last two years of his life. Now he was gone, and I missed him terribly. I also had a drinking problem. I wanted to move far away from my grief and my problems and just start over. Since I'd always liked the Gulf of Mexico area, I decided to move somewhere near there. Why not? I packed up my things and my two cats and headed south.

Grandpa and I had acquired two male house cats when I was living with him. I named the big fourteen-pound Maine coon after Grandpa, whose name was Lowell Bernard. We called the cat by his initials, L. B., but wound up spelling it Elbee. The cat was all white with blue eyes, and as is the case with most blue-eyed white cats, he was deaf. He had excellent eye contact, though, and he understood my gestures for *come, get down,* even *bad boy.* He was a nice, laid-back cat.

I asked Grandpa to name the other cat, and he named him after my initials of M. O. Moe was a gorgeous twelve-pound caramel tiger with gold eyes that seemed to match his coat. He also was a scaredy-cat by nature.

Of course, you take yourself wherever you go. But I made the move to Mississippi with high hopes. I found a nice mobile home not far from Biloxi that sat in a lush, green clearing surrounded by pine woods and large mature oak trees with a creek nearby. It was lovely.

I enjoyed the Gulf area right away. I started going to school. And of course I loved walking the beaches. That's where, on a sunny day in Bay St. Louis, I met the man I'll call Mark. Somehow he recognized in me a fellow alcoholic. We talked for hours there on the beach, where he convinced me there was a better life. Mark took me to my first Alcoholics Anonymous meeting in New Orleans. I soon got sober and started my recovery. Life was better, just as Mark had said.

Eventually Mark and I were dating. I had been living in the area for less than a year and had been sober for only ninety days when I heard that Hurricane Katrina was on its way. I'd never been in a hurricane before, so I took the evacuation order seriously. When the radio announcer listed the things to have on hand in preparation, I wrote it all down.

I lived about an hour from New Orleans, and Mark lived in the Gentilly section of New Orleans, right near the Ninth Ward. He didn't intend to leave the city—he was more casual about tropical storms, as were most people there, and the storm was only supposed to last three days. He laughed at my nervous and naïve Yankee ways, but I managed to talk him into leaving town. We decided to drive to the Florida panhandle and weather the storm with some friends there. About ten of us would gather at someone's condo to sit things out and enjoy each other's company. That's the New Orleans way.

Mark drove to my place and parked his car, and we packed my Ford Focus with the things we would need. As I said, this was my first hurricane, so I was doing everything the radio told me to do. Mark continued to laugh at me. Then he started getting annoyed as he watched me pack flashlights, canned goods, a tent, charcoal, a transistor radio, and blankets, ticking off my list as I packed.

Of course I took Mo and Elbee. No way would I leave my cats home for three days, especially in a hurricane. So there was another checklist: kitty litter, cat food, dishes, blankets—I even packed leashes for them. Once Mark realized I was taking the cats, he let me know he thought I was being silly. But I had no intention of leaving my cats to fly away to the land of Oz.

It wasn't that Mark disliked cats. He had been feeding a stray at his house for quite some time. It was a feral black cat who wouldn't allow anyone to touch or pet him, but Mark could coax him onto his porch to feed him cat food out of the can. The cat had an unusual habit where he would dip his paw into the wet food and eat right off his paw. But Mark wasn't concerned about the stray cat. After all, this was only going to be a three-day deal, and a feral cat would do just fine for that length of time.

So the car was packed and off we went, east to Florida—and straight into an unbelievable traffic jam. We had expected to get to our destination in five hours, but Alabama was bumper to bumper, so it turned into a fifteen-hour trip. By the time we got to the condo the night before the storm hit land, it was already mighty windy. Elbee and Mo handled the ride pretty well, and once we got to the condo I kept them confined to one room. They were fine, all things considered, and we enjoyed a nice evening with friends.

The storm hit the next day, and we lost power very soon. Cell calls were sporadic; I was never able to contact my family up north. We were on the east side of the hurricane, the side that traditionally absorbs the worst impact, and Mark and I were starting to realize that this probably wasn't the best place to be. But being with friends had sounded good to us, plus our hostess was a nice grandmotherly woman we all had wanted to keep an eye on.

I'd never been through anything like this hurricane. It was only the edge of the storm, but it was loud and dark. We heard lots of banging outside so we stayed away from windows. That night everyone tried to sleep, but throughout the night the guests would get up and wander around in the dark, checking things out. The cats stayed hidden and very still, huddled in survival mode.

It was a long night, but the next morning we had the impression the worst was over. We gathered around the transistor radio I'd packed and listened to the news about the levees in New Orleans. I looked at Mark's face and could tell that something horrible was happening. "That levee is where I live," he said. I didn't understand the city's layout that well, but Mark knew water was pouring into his neighborhood, which was adjacent to the Ninth Ward.

Three days later, Mark and I were both antsy to leave the condo and get back to our own homes. We were able to start up the water-logged car, so we packed it and headed out, glad to get moving.

It didn't take long to realize that we had a new set of problems. There was no power anywhere, so there was no gas available and there were no ATMs. Few people were out and about. Trees were down and roads were closed. There was no clear path to get home. I had packed an atlas, so we found alternate routes, but unfortunately this roaming around wasted gas at a time when no gas stations were open. It became apparent we were going to have to stay over somewhere.

For three nights I slept in the Focus with the cats, and Mark slept on the ground. We found gas rationed out at five gallons at a time. We'd sit in gas lines that moved so slowly that sometimes I'd put leashes on the cats and take them for little strolls while Mark crawled along in the car. We'd gas up, then use all that gas looking for the next gas station. It was three steps forward, two steps back. Waiting in line at one gas station, we could hear what sounded like a gunshot up the road. It turned out that someone had been siphoning gas out of a pickup truck, and the truck's owner shot and killed him. It was horrible.

Mark was getting more and more anxious. He knew his house was flooded, and it was wearing on him. The shooting unnerved us both, and now the cats were acting up, which was in turn annoying Mark. This was not a good situation. It went on for three days until we got to Laurel, Mississippi.

In Laurel we found a church parking lot where a very nice young pastor—Brother Ken—invited us to be safe and stay there in the parking lot. I pitched the tent, and suddenly both Mo and Elbee started yowling inside it. I grabbed the flashlight and discovered I had pitched the tent on an anthill. Ants were biting the cats and everything else. So we pulled things apart, and the cats and I slept in the car another night. Mark rolled out his bedroll on the ground away from the ants.

We wound up staying in Laurel for a full week, camped out in the parking lot of Brother Ken's church. It was hot and steamy and miserable. But Brother Ken was wonderful, and so were his parishioners. He brought us Bibles and he prayed with us; I credit this pastor for saving Mark's sanity during this time. Brother Ken kept a chainsaw in his truck, which he'd use to get around the fallen trees to check on his parishioners. Those gracious people brought us food. There was no power the entire time. We had to go to the bathroom in the woods, and we accessed water through a hose behind the church that was fed by a water tower across the street simply through the force of gravity.

Eventually the military arrived with ready-made meals (MREs). Then FEMA showed up and passed out bottles of water. They didn't want to give me water for the cats, so I shared my ration of water with my boys.

By now it was two weeks since we'd left home, and Mark and I decided to try again. We packed up and said good-bye to Brother Ken. Mark wanted to go straight to the city, but I insisted we go to my place first and get his car. So off we went.

At this point the cats had had enough. They refused to use the cat box in the car, so I was taking them outside. Then I ran out of food for them. We still had trouble traveling because of closed roads and lack of power, but fortunately along the way we came upon a mom-and-pop convenience store. Although they were out of gas, they had cat food—and I bought every bit of it.

From the church it would take a day and a half to get home, a distance that should have taken two hours. Then, only fifty miles from my house, we ran out of gas. We stayed in that car one more miserable night with doors and windows open until a gas station opened at daylight.

When we finally got to my house, I was amazed and grateful to find it still standing and intact. It was obvious that the wind had tried to take my mobile home off its moorings, and all the many mature trees were down and strewn around the property, yet somehow none of them fell on my house or on Mark's car.

Mark drove off for New Orleans to learn that his house was, as he feared, being destroyed by floodwater. He couldn't get anywhere near it, so he lived with friends for a few weeks. He'd lost everything and felt simply adrift. This whole experience had strained our relationship, but we remained friends and stayed in touch by phone. We'd gone through that awful trip together, and that gave us a bond that kept us concerned for one another.

It took two months for the New Orleans water to recede enough for Mark to drive to his house. I was in town that day, and I went with him. It was a total loss. The water lines were ten feet high inside, and there were marks on the outside of the house from the search-and-rescue people. Mark would not be moving back in anytime soon.

The next time I was around, we drove over to the house again. We heard a yowling coming from the garage, and sure enough, there was a cat in the rafters—a black one. Mark thought it looked like the stray he'd left behind, but it would be hard to know for sure. Was it the stray? Did he survive the flood on the roof? Had he been living in the rafters all this time?

Mark put a can of cat food out before he left, and he continued to leave food on the porch whenever he came by. Something was eating it. Finally one day he was able to see the black cat approach the food on the porch. The cat dipped his paw in the can and ate off it. What a survivor. It was one happy ending in the middle of a lot of misery.

Back at my place, Mo and Elbee were glad to be in their own home, though they didn't like to be left alone anymore. I would have no power or water for another six weeks. I had to use the creek for bathing and for water for the cats. It was scary watching out for reptiles while doing that, and now there was a pack of wild dogs wandering the neighborhood. But we remained safe.

It's many years later. I live back up north near my grown children and grandchildren. I no longer have my Moe or Elbee. But by the grace of God, I am still sober.

# For the Love of Sandy

*Jill Eileen Smith*

When my sister was about eight years old, my parents promised her a puppy. But a few months later they told her she was going to have a little brother or sister. So instead of a puppy, she got me.

Eventually, my parents did get the dog she'd hoped for, a little black terrier who ended up sleeping on my bed at night after my sister got married. That dog remained with my parents long after I moved out, the only dog I ever claimed as a pet. Since then, my husband, Randy, and I have been a cat family.

Our first cat, Sandy, joined us during our first year of marriage and remained a family member for twenty-one years. He was a handsome pale-orange tabby—hence the name Sandy. When people think of cats, they often think of aloof animals who don't come when called and who consider their owners as household staff meant to care for them. Dogs, on the other hand, are grateful to be fed, obedient (when trained), and loyal.

Sandy was more like a dog in kitty attire.

Dogs love unconditionally. Sandy loved unconditionally. He greeted us when we came home from work, slept on our bed at night but didn't disturb us, and seemed to sense when we needed comfort. He was patient with children and loved to wrestle with Randy. When he saw a claw-like hand covered in an old flannel shirt ready to attack, he went after it with gusto.

When our nieces and nephews picked him up and carried him around like a rag doll, he never fought to get free, though sometimes he looked like he wouldn't mind if play time ended. He never hissed or bit, even when manhandled. He seemed to know that his handlers were children, and he had a gentle way about him in their presence.

Of course, Sandy was still a cat. He had no front claws, but we would allow him to go into the backyard as long as we were watching him. One summer day I was in the kitchen and Sandy was in the yard. He came to the back glass door, proudly holding a small bird in his mouth as if to say, "Look what I caught!"

It is possible I overreacted. (I thought the bird was dead!) But Sandy didn't seem to want to worry me, so he opened his mouth and the bird flew away. I think he'd grown tired of those birds sitting on the fence taunting him, and he wanted to let them know that he was faster than they thought. Just because he didn't have front claws didn't mean he couldn't catch them. Those birds thought twice about teasing him again.

Another time he found some baby mice in the yard (we had a field behind us where they seemed to breed). I came upon him batting something around the yard, and I'm sure to him he was just playing. But he played so hard, the poor thing didn't survive. I honestly don't think he meant to hurt the baby mouse. He just was thrilled to have a toy that moved all on its own, even if he didn't touch it.

So Sandy did let us know in these ways and more that he was all cat and proud of it. But he still had the affectionate heart that most people associate with dogs. The most touching way he proved that to me was when I miscarried our first child.

I had struggled for about a year with infertility. The hardest part came when I watched friends and family members having babies and month after month I did not conceive. Then that happy day came that I became pregnant! We were thrilled! But our joy was short-lived. Sixteen weeks later I suffered a miscarriage. I was beside myself with grief.

Sometimes we underestimate how much it hurts for a woman to suffer a miscarriage. It is not like there is a funeral and a gathering of friends to help us grieve. Though I will say, friends and family were very kind to us and sent sympathy cards and offered prayers on our behalf during that time. We felt very loved.

And yet, I still grieved. I remember one particular day when the tears were fresh and the pain so raw. I lay on the couch and cried and cried. Through my tears, I sensed a presence beside me. Sandy came near, cautiously at first, as though he was not sure what to do. He tilted his head to look at me, as if to say, "Are you okay?" And then he jumped onto my lap and loved me. He let me hold him tight and cry into his fur. He did not try to get away but settled with me, comforting me.

Sandy's love helped me heal.

I let my maternal instincts fall on him for a time after that moment. One time when he went outside, I couldn't find him and nearly panicked. I couldn't bear to lose him. Sandy had a habit of hiding in the neighbor's bushes where he enjoyed rubbing noses with the dog next door. This time, he had traveled halfway around the block before we found him. But he came home and settled right in, not the least perturbed that we had scolded him for going so far.

As Sandy aged, and we did, too, we welcomed three new sons into our home (several years apart). Sandy would look at us each time as if to ask, "So we have another?" But he accepted each one, and as they grew up, he let them drag him around the house just like he had our nieces and nephews when he was younger.

Sandy lived with us a very long time. Looking back on pictures, I am always surprised at how young he once looked. By his senior years, his fur had grown flatter, his frame thinner, and he snuggled close to us to stay warm more than to comfort us. Our love for each other had come full circle. In the end, of course, even love could not keep him, and the day came when we had to say good-bye to this pet who had made our lives richer by his presence, by his cat antics, by his love.

The next day we headed for the Humane Society and adopted another cat, Shadow. Six years later we added Tiger to our family. Both have taught us many things about sibling rivalry, about how to play, but most of all, like Sandy before them, about the unconditional nature of love.

### When Kitty Has a Hitch in Her Git-along . . .

Housecats live longer lives these days, which means they can get the same kinds of aging issues we humans get. If you notice your aging cat is having a little trouble getting around or hisses more when touched, she may be having some arthritis problems. First, of course, see your vet for a diagnosis. Sometimes there is medication that can help. Many more vets now are using acupuncture or chiropractic manipulation on cats. Some natural things to try are fish oil, which has been found to be a pain reliever in both cats and dogs, and glucosamine sprinkled into wet food. At home, make sure kitty has easier ways of getting on and off the things she used to easily clamber around. Pet stairs work, of course. Also check out yard sales, resale shops, and craft stores for inexpensive stepping stools you can place all around the house.

# The Monk Goes on Retreat

*Robert Benson*

A creature known as the Monk lives at our house. Though she is dressed in black and white—polka dots, no less— she is not actually a monk, she is a cat. There are people who say she is cute. I say the jury is still out. She is likely withholding judgment on me, as well.

The Monk has a real name, a name that is on her papers and in her file at the veterinarian, and she has a couple of other nicknames to boot, but Monk is the name we call her most often.

I have never thought of myself as a cat person, but the Monk largely pays no attention to my position on the matter. She adopted me as her person some years ago. My cries to the contrary went ignored, lost in the language barrier that is a fixture of our relationship. It is a strange and wonderful relationship. One of us is strange, one of us is wonderful.

She follows me around as though she is a puppy, she watches me work as though she is earning a living, and she wakes me up in the morning as though she is needed somewhere each day.

Between the two of us, we are nothing more and nothing less than a writer and a cat. Neither of which is actually necessary to the quality of life on the planet.

And only one of us is particularly very good at what we were put on the planet to be.

Besides being a writer, I am a very serious, very card-carrying Episcopalian, though I did not grow up that way.

I grew up in a much less formal religious crowd, a very devout group to be sure, but not a place where ancient traditions were practiced. The church crowd I grew up in did not burn incense or ring bells, employ collared clerics or white-robed acolytes, chant psalms or offer confessions, make fasts or mark feasts or any such things.

The places I grew up in did not use the word *monk* very often, either. *Monk* was a Catholic sort of word.

And Lord knows we did not haul our animals to church to have them blessed on the Feast of St. Francis, as is the practice at the Cathedral where I now proudly flash my aforementioned Episcopalian card. Every year, at the Feast of Saint Francis, horses and birds and dogs and hamsters and all manner of other creatures are brought in to be blessed. A horse that works for the police department generally leads the parade, right through the front door and down the center aisle while a processional hymn is sung. Every year a dog bites the priest who is making the sign of the cross on its forehead.

Man, did we who grew up as something other than Episcopalians miss a show.

We have never taken the Monk to the Cathedral for the blessing of the animals. I asked her once if she wanted to go.

No kidding, I asked her, as though she was going to understand and then answer me. We sat at the top of the steps, just in front of the door to my upstairs studio, and she paid very careful attention to every word I said. Or at least she looked like she did. How does a non-cat-person know whether a cat can understand the question?

She looked at me as though any idiot knows that there is no need for a monastic to attend a ceremony of blessing authorized and conducted by mere humans. Why would such a creature need a blessing from a mere priest?

Though I write about the contemplative life and the Monk watches me do so while she is lounging on my desk or in the window seat across the room, we do not really talk much about religion.

I expect she has her suspicions about my faith, or lack thereof, and I have my own suspicions about hers. My concern about the ongoing spiritual value of my work probably matters little to her. She is much more concerned about the white space in her kibble bowl than anything else. Our mutual skepticism toward the central issue in the other's life is a respectful one.

I have long suspected that the Monk is a pagan, which is why I was so startled when she took to joining me when I said prayers early in the morning.

Not too long ago, the sweet woman who was kind and generous enough to marry me had to be away for a week or so. A few days and a few nights to myself seemed to be an opportunity for a kind of stay-at-home retreat.

*Stay-cations* hold no interest for me—an actual vacation can only take place on an actual beach. But a *stay-retreat* seemed intriguing to me somehow.

I took the phone off the hook, ignored all mail (be it from the technophiles or the snails), and cooked and consumed all of my meals in the quiet and privacy and glory of my own home.

A quiet broken only by the insistent callings of the Monk.

As part of my ritual for my retreat, I said the daily office, a set of ancient and formal prayers that have been a part of the Christian tradition since the very beginning of the Christian tradition. Indeed, the roots of the prayers reach back into Hebrew practice. I have been saying the office one way or another for a long time, generally in solitude, in silence.

My mentioning this is not to be construed as a sign of anything much in the category of devotion. I bring it up only so that I can tell you that the difference during my stay-retreat is that I said the prayers in our front parlor and I said them aloud.

Which is not the cat part of the story. (Unless the Furry One Who Lives In Our House was actually around when David wrote the Psalms.)

The cat part of the story is this: Each day during that retreat, when I rang the bell and lit the candle and started the incense and began to chant aloud, the Monk would come and sit facing me across the little table I had designated as my altar for the week. Four times a day, every time I rang the bell, she came running and took her place in the, dare I say it, choir.

She would look me in the eye the entire time and sing at the top of her lungs. Or wail or meow or whatever it is that furry monastics call that noise they make.

It took a bit to get used to saying the *Our Father* with a cat singing a descant. But I finally stopped giggling and went back to praying.

The Monk shows up on my side of the bed now just as the sun comes up, a good hour before the alarm goes off, and begins to call to me early in the morning.

The sweet woman to whom I am married says the Monk is just singing. She could be right. Though having said yes to marrying me, the woman's judgment is clearly in question—not her kindness, God knows—her judgment. (Either way, my gratitude is never ending.)

When I get tired of the Monk's wake-up song, I get out of bed and head upstairs. She runs up the stairs ahead of me and is sitting in front of the little table we two used as a common altar that week.

The Monk may be joining in a morning hymn none of the rest of us can quite hear.

But it could be the Monk is calling me to prayer.

It could be she is willing to take me to the Cathedral for the Feast of Saint Francis and stand beside me while I am blessed.

---

### Back in the Day

There were no house cats in ancient Rome or Greece, and there is also no specific reference to domestic cats in the Bible. It was the Egyptians who took on the task of domesticating the cat into something similar to our house cat, and it took them around a thousand years to do that, far longer than it has taken man to domesticate any other animal. So are we cat lovers surprised?[3]

# The Stepcat

*Kathi Lipp*

M y husband and I thought we would be the exceptions to the rule.

We had heard the statistics about blended families, but we thought we would have an edge. After all, Roger and I had known each other for years, and my kids loved Roger and his kids loved me.

That is, until we told them we were getting married. That's when I went from being someone Jeremy, my future stepson, loved, to public enemy number one. Jeremy wanted nothing to do with me or my kids. He hated the fact that he had to share a room with my son, Justen. He hated that we were moving in on his turf. He distanced himself in every way from us that he could find.

To complicate matters, in addition to blending our two families, I was bringing another issue into our marriage: our adopted cat, Zorro.

Zorro was the kitten my kids and I rescued from our local shelter during one of the hardest times of our lives. I knew that we needed a rough and tumble cat who could keep up with my kids and our golden retriever, Einstein. So when I saw Zorro curled up in a little black-and-white fluff ball in the corner of the kitten room at the shelter, I passed him up, thinking he was a little too gentle for our family. But when one of his siblings nudged him to play, Zorro pounced on him like a tiger stalking his prey in the wilds of Africa. I knew that Zorro would be able to hold his own in our home.

We got him home, and it took no time for Zorro to put his new seventy-pound brother, Einstein, in his place. Zorro ruled the house, and we all knew it. If there was a particularly desirable patch of sun where Einstein had curled up, it only took one swipe of a paw from Zorro to let our dog know that it was time for him to go to the shady corner of the sunroom so that the reigning animal could claim his rightful place.

Yes, Zorro was something of a bully. But he was our bully, and my kids and I loved him, and he was as much a part of our family as any of the humans.

But sadly, Zorro had not been in my future husband's life plan.

Roger had never seen himself as a cat owner. In fact, when we got engaged, he asked my mom (whom I was living with at the time) if she would be willing to keep Zorro after we got married. Zorro didn't get along with my mom's Maine coon, Jenny, so my mom was firm: "You get the girl—you get the cat." Roger was defiantly not wild about Zorro. So of course, Zorro couldn't get enough of Roger.

Zorro would wait by the front door for Roger to get home in the evenings. As soon as Roger crossed the threshold, there was the black-and-white drill sergeant barking orders. Zorro was insistent that Roger head upstairs and lay down for a nap. A few minutes after Roger arrived home, I would go upstairs to find Zorro tucked under Roger's arm, both of them snoring lightly. So while Zorro and Roger had successfully "blended," the rest of the family was having a harder time.

My stepson, Jeremy, continued to be moody and disrespectful—to both me and his dad. He would sulk through the house, snapping at anyone who dared speak to him. Jeremy would spend hours hitting hockey pucks in our garage to take out his aggressions. He was not happy with any of us, and with the *Slap! . . . Slap! . . . Slap!* of the hockey pucks, he made sure we knew it.

Jeremy couldn't even stand Zorro. When Jer had a group of his friends over one afternoon, one of the kids saw Zorro and said, "Dude, I didn't know you had a cat." And Jeremy, without even looking up, said, "I don't. That's the stepcat." He was mad at everyone. Even Zorro.

It was a frustrating situation to be sure. And it was becoming exhausting. Jeremy was up late night after night, venting his frustration by going on long, late walks with his dad or taking out his aggression on mul-tiple hockey pucks. Which would have been fine, except someone else had become a very early riser: Zorro.

Our cat had taken to waking up at 5:14 (not 5:13 or 5:15 mind you—5:14) and screeching at an ear-piercing decibel. He stood in the middle of the hall and bellowed for twenty minutes every single morning. We tried feeding him. We tried letting him into our room. We tried threatening him by cutting out one of his nine lives. Nothing helped.

This went on for months, Jeremy's late nights and Zorro's early mornings. I was concerned that Roger was considering returning both the cat and me to my mom.

And then, all of the sudden, it all came to an end. Jeremy stopped staying up late and Zorro stopping playing rooster in our hallway. We were scared to ask too many questions. We just thanked God and slept in until 6:45.

When one morning Jeremy forgot to set his alarm, the mystery was solved. I couldn't believe my eyes when I went into his room. There Jeremy was with Zorro the stepcat perched on top of him. Come to find out, Zorro had been sleeping on (not next to, but on) Jeremy for the last several months. Every night Zorro would push his way into Jeremy's room and sleep there lazily until morning.

When our family was at its worst, Zorro picked out the person who needed him most and claimed him as his own. Jeremy wanted nothing to do with his new family, but he could only resist his stepcat for so long.

Even now, when Jeremy, who has been living on his own for a couple of years, comes over to visit, Zorro wastes no time claiming Jeremy as his very own. As soon as Jeremy sits down, Zorro is on top of him, purring happily that his boy is back.

*big cat in deep sleep*
*comes awake daybreak and dawn*
*predator house cat*

# Cat from the Land Between

*Pamela Allnutt*

Steamy warmth wrapped itself around me as I sat on the front stoop, a cup of coffee in hand. The muffled *whoosh* of cars from the nearby highway mixed with the sounds of trilling birds. Children migrated from yard to yard, their moms' watchful eyes tracking them from windows and porches. Leafy trees lined the narrow street. I breathed in the earthy smells of growing plants in wet earth and let myself be lulled. It had been a tough year.

From these steps I had watched the child we were trying to adopt adjust to his new surroundings and play for the past year. It was here that he proudly learned to ride a two-wheeler. It was here that he pretended to be a superhero, wearing home-made Batman and Spiderman costumes while trailing behind our older son, imitating his every move. Behind those idyllic images, though, was a darker story.

My husband and I had started the process a year before the child arrived, filling out forms and being interviewed. We were then placed on a waiting list for an "older child with special needs." This was the plan we had long held dear: to have one biological child and adopt the next. The beautiful boy we were matched with was labeled a "legal risk," meaning that there were still some issues to be worked out before the adoption could go through. Nevertheless, the caseworker encouraged us, believing these details could be resolved.

However, there were weekly disruptions. These included talks with our lawyer, the birth mother, the caseworker, and later, a child psychologist. Just as it seemed that we had conquered one problem, the situation would morph and another glitch would appear to challenge and frustrate us. Finally, after twelve months of caring for this child and hoping to blend as a family, our lawyer told us there was no way we would be able to adopt him. And then he was gone.

His empty bedroom echoed with bruised memories. Tattered dreams hung in the air.

We were also facing a move soon, to another state. I was already in mourning for the friends we would leave behind, those who had become so close during our years in this neighborhood and especially through the trials of the past year.

A muffled cry startled me out of my mental fog. It seemed to have come from a line of scraggly hostas spanning the narrow gap between our house and the next. Putting down my coffee cup, I descended the steps and parted the wide leaves. A young cat, about half grown, crouched in the shadows, its mottled black and brown fur a good camouflage. She must have come from between the houses.

"Well, hello!" I said, reaching out slowly. After sniffing my hand, she crept from her hiding place and arched her bony back beneath my palm, purring. Her golden eyes locked with mine, as though memorizing my features.

It wasn't long before she followed me up the steps, bumping her face hard against my bare legs, circling them over and over. She wasn't wild, so perhaps she lived in the neighborhood. I asked the children passing by if she was theirs or looked familiar, but no one recognized her.

"Will she be all right?" my six-year-old son asked, his brow furrowed.

"Well, she looks pretty healthy to me and doesn't seem to be afraid of people, so she probably has a home. I think she's just visiting," I assured him, trying to put aside my own concerns for her.

"Go on now, your family will be worried about you," I told the cat.

Turning, I went inside to get on with my day, putting loads of laundry through their cycles and making grilled cheese sandwiches for lunch. A trip to my son's favorite park, the one with the old train engine to climb on, rounded out the afternoon. The cat was forgotten in the evening scramble of supper, bath time, and stories.

The next morning, a favorite game was taking place in the shadowed strip of dirt between the houses—the same territory where the cat had emerged from the day before. Armed with battered spoons, my son and his friends were pretending to be archaeologists like Indiana Jones, digging in the rocky soil for traces of past civilizations. They had often found treasures there: a mysterious piece of metal, a shard of pottery from some long-gone dish or cup, even a small bleached animal bone. Today, a chipped marble and a tiny letter once belonging to a Lego mailman were unearthed. They had struck it big!

As soon as I stepped out on the porch to check on the explorers, the cat appeared. Coming again from the hostas bordering the archaeological dig, it was apparent she had been waiting for me. She ran up the steps to greet me, purring loudly. "Well, hello again!" I said, bending down to scratch her chin. I had secretly hoped to see her. She was starting to grow on me.

Soon, however, I returned to the house to write out my grocery list and do some cleaning. When I checked throughout the day, she was still there, waiting patiently. Moved by her persistence, I finally opened the screen door and invited her in.

It did not go well.

Ernie, our beautiful but antisocial cat, showed her displeasure by issuing a series of long hisses accompanied by a fearsome arched back. Cowed, the adolescent visitor crawled under the sofa for safety. Her triangular chin and wide eyes peeked out from the edge of the upholstery skirt. She dared not move.

There had been too much drama in the past year, and it just didn't seem like the right time to add another member to our family. So I fed our guest and then put her outside for the night.

The next morning I stepped out on the porch to visit with Angie, my neighbor from across the street. As we talked, I looked around—no cat in sight. Feeling slightly relieved as well as a bit apprehensive, I wondered if she was okay . . . after all, there was a busy road nearby.

Suddenly, a piercing wail came from above.

We looked up, and there she stood, balanced on the edge of the neighboring rooftop. "How on earth did she get up there?" I wondered aloud. It was as though she had deliberately staked out a better position to get my attention.

It worked. I tried to figure out what to do. She continued yowling, directing her complaints pointedly at me. Stepping down from the porch, I called to her in a soft voice, walking backward slowly between the houses, skirting the holes from the archaeological dig. She followed me to the back of the house, retracing the route she must have taken earlier.

Cocking her head, she listened intently as I coaxed her to jump down onto the back porch overhang and then to the stair railing leading to the back yard.

She considered, looking back and forth from me to the distance below. She jumped once and then again. My heart leaped with her. As soon as she landed on the ground, she ran to greet me, bonking her head on my legs. Greatly relieved, I stooped to pick her up. She put a paw on either side of my neck and rubbed her chin to mine.

I was hooked.

There was no mistake. This cat had chosen me to be her special person and our home as her home in spite of the roadblocks both Ernie and I had put up. She walked confidently ahead of me up the steps to the back door of our house. As I opened it, she whisked inside, her tail a jaunty flag.

She never looked back. Named Frisky, she soon made the move with us to our new home, bringing a playful and loving spirit along with her. After a while, she even parlayed a sort of peace with Ernie. We were a family.

The painful fog that enveloped me on that long-ago morning gradually lifted, and from the distance of years, the memory of that brave cat still shines. She was the real treasure to come out of that barren strip of ground between the houses at just the right time. She helped me to move on from the shadowy mind-set of failure and loss to one of acceptance and into the brilliant freedom to love again.

# The Cat Doesn't Even Like the Dog

## Donna Acton

I met Louine when I was fifteen and she was sixty-five years old. She was just the nicest person. She hired me to clean her house when her car was rear-ended, causing her whiplash. This was the third time in a year that Louine's car had been rear-ended. Because of her injury, she couldn't look up or look down or raise her arms. I was hired, three days a week after school, to clean everything in her house above and below her line of sight.

Louine and her husband, Chalmers, lived just up the street from my father's veterinary hospital. We never saw much of Chalmers, but Louine was a constant fixture in our office. Through the years, all of her pets had been our patients, and since I had been working in the veterinary hospital from the age of eight, I had seen and talked to Louine many, many times.

My only other job was baby-sitting, which I started when I was twelve years old. But working for your family and baby-sitting didn't seem to qualify as real jobs. Being hired by Louine did.

Mostly she gave me art lessons in the basement with oil paints, and we made candles by pouring hot wax over crushed ice in milk cartons. Louine always worked with her gray hair pulled into a tight bun with gray bobby pins, and she wore floral aprons decorated with rickrack. She worked in many art media. One time she created an abstract piece of stained glass. The circle of deep red represented the burning bush, the blue glass was the Sea of Galilee, and the sandy brown glass portrayed the desert wildness. The colors swirled into a wonderful mosaic of color even before you held it up to the window.

While working for Louine I also learned how to blanch green beans for canning and how to make ham croquets with sauce for her ladies' luncheons and church circle. When the weather was warm I would weed her flower garden and fall asleep behind the tall gladiolas in the summer sun. Here in Michigan we don't take sunny days lightly. We adore them because they are so rare. The Great Lakes protect us from the wild swings of weather ranging from below zero to above 100 degrees, but the protection comes in the form of cloud cover and leaden gray skies that go on for days, weeks, and months.

One afternoon, as I washed the matching glass plates and tea cups, Louine gave me a piece of advice that has served me well over the years. When I unloaded the dishwasher, my hand slipped and I broke one of her grandmother's rose-patterned teacups. I was devastated. I couldn't apologize enough.

But Louine informed me that I didn't need to feel so bad. "People are more important than things," she said. In the years since, whenever someone has accidently broken or destroyed something that held a great value to me, I remember Louine's words, and I learned how to forgive others because she had forgiven me.

Louine and Chalmers's daughter, Margie, rescued a beagle–German shepherd mix, named her Missy, and then promptly moved to Arizona for a new job. She left Missy with her folks. Louine and Chalmers weren't opposed to having a dog, but Pumpkin, their big orange cat, was totally against the idea. Pumpkin loved Chalmers, who was a dentist with a very hectic practice. When he got home from the office each evening, he sat in his big chair and smoked his pipe to relax. Each evening Pumpkin would settle on Chalmers's lap and purr as the smoke from Chalmers's pipe drifted up and around the two of them.

But Louine was worried about Missy. "Do you think she will miss Margie?"

"No," I said. "Not like you think she will. Missy will always remember Margie, but she will bond with you and your husband after just a few days of living with you."

Whenever Missy strayed into what Pumpkin believed to be his personal space, Pumpkin puffed up the fur on his tail, hissed, and slashed at Missy's face with his claws. Missy learned to give Pumpkin a wide berth, and Pumpkin spent most of his time ignoring Missy, pretending she didn't even live there. To Pumpkin, Missy became the invisible dog.

Then Louine felt sorry for Missy. "Do you think they'll ever be friends?"

"Maybe someday," I said. "Mostly Pumpkin will just tolerate Missy, but Missy will never stop trying to get Pumpkin to like her."

One day new neighbors moved in next door. They owned a big Siberian husky named Apollo, who was chained in the backyard. The new neighbors said it was a short-term solution until they got their yard fenced in. Louine found all this out when she delivered a casserole to their back door with a card that said "Welcome to the Neighborhood." She was that kind of person. I learned about the joy of giving from her.

Missy, deciding to do her own welcome, went through the hedgerow of squat lilac bushes and tall pine trees separating the two backyards to say hi to Apollo, who immediately barked and growled at her. Missy came running home, her tail tucked between her legs.

Louine told me that Apollo got loose every once in a while in the evening when they were taking him into the house. She said he didn't look very friendly. I told her the fence posts were already in place and the neighbor's fence would be erected soon.

The very next day, Louine greeted me as I walked up her driveway after school.

"You won't believe what happened," she said. "Both Missy and Pumpkin were in the backyard with me in the garden. I was picking dill weed. Of course Pumpkin was watching from her usual spot under the rhododendron bush. That big Apollo from next door came charging through the hedgerow and went right after Missy. It just scared her to pieces. It scared *me* to pieces!"

"Is Missy okay?" I asked.

Louine nodded. "Right when I thought it was curtains for poor Missy, Pumpkin came charging out from his hiding spot and jumped on Apollo's head. The dog shook and shook and pawed at his head, but Pumpkin wouldn't turn him loose. That cat just dug his claws in deeper and was biting that dog's face. Finally, Apollo hightailed it back to his own yard with Pumpkin latched on to his head."

"Is Pumpkin okay?" I asked.

"Oh, yes. They're both just fine," she said. "About ten minutes later I saw Pumpkin sitting next to the maple tree, taking a bath, smoothing all his fur back into place."

We walked indoors to the kitchen and looked through the window at the garden. "I have a question," Louine said. "Pumpkin doesn't seem to even like Missy, so why would he attack that big Apollo and protect her?"

It only took me a moment to think of how to explain it to her. I learned it from my father in the exam room of our hospital. He had a way of connecting with people and getting his point or information across to them. I knew I could explain this to Louine through football. In East Lansing, Michigan, is Michigan State University, and in Ann Arbor is the University of Michigan.

"You have to think of Missy and Pumpkin like Michigan and Michigan State," I said. "They do not like each other at all. That is, until they play Ohio State. Apollo is Ohio State."

Pumpkin strode through the kitchen to his dish, ignoring Missy as usual, meowing loudly, demanding to be fed. Louine looked at him adoringly as she opened a can of his favorite cat food and scooped a heaping mound into his dish.

"I see," Louine said. "That makes perfect sense. You're so good at explaining those things to me." Then she turned for the basement door. "Now, before you start your cleaning, let's go downstairs and work on that pencil sketch for your watercolor. I've got everything ready for us. After your art lesson, I'll show you how to can dill pickles."

Apollo never made a return visit to Louine's backyard. The fence went up quickly the next day. Every once in a while you could catch a glimpse of Apollo peering tentatively through the fence and the hedge, but the mere sight of Pumpkin would cause him to duck his head away. As for Pumpkin, he stayed on his side of the fence, hunkered down under the rhododendron bush, watching.

### Get Thee to a Veterinarian

It's an odd and unfortunate fact: More dogs than cats are seen regularly by a vet—yet more people have cats than have dogs. In America, 82 million people have cats while 72 million have dogs, yet cats see the veterinarian only about half as frequently as dogs. That's a shame. If we want kitty to live a long and healthy life, we need to take him in for his wellness exams on a regular basis. It's worth it. Besides, why let the dogs win this one?[4]

# Cool Cat, School Cat

### Ed Peterson

The year was 1967—a year filled with turbulence both nationally and internationally. And yet, at the same time, possibilities seemed endless. These were the days when a generation answered President Kennedy's call to work for the poor, and I was one of that generation. After college graduation, I left my small-town, middle-class world and took a job teaching fourth grade in an urban school in Flint, Michigan. This was in the fall immediately following the summer riots in nearby Detroit.

Not only were changes afoot all over the world, they were also afoot in education. The word *relevance* was big then. We teachers were trying new things in the classroom to make education meaningful and fun for students. These were the days when curriculum was freer, and we could try novel things in teaching—even take the kids and a guitar outside to sit under a tree and teach folk songs. They were exciting years to me.

One day during my rookie year at the Flint school, my students found an injured cat on the playground. He was a half-grown tiger with a gash on his leg. Another teacher and I decided the cat should go to the vet and we'd split the cost. The cat spent the night at the vet, and fortunately the doctor gave us a good deal as he treated the cat's infection and gave him his shots. The next day, my colleague picked the cat up from the vet, but he brought him to school because he didn't know anyone who wanted the cat. I didn't feel I should have a cat at my apartment because I was a single man who was at school more than I was home, so somehow I got the idea that I'd just keep the cat in the classroom. Like I said, these were the days when you could do more unusual things at school.

Of course, I needed permission to do this. We had a good principal who was kind to this rookie teacher. He asked a number of questions, such as who would take care of the cat and what would happen to him on the weekend. Once I answered to his satisfaction, the principal said I could have the cat in my classroom as long as it stayed there and didn't roam the halls.

I sent a note home to parents advising them that there would be a classroom cat, and if they had a problem with that, please talk to me. Some parents would come in to see the cat out of curiosity, but none of them had a problem with him being there.

The first day that the cat joined us in class, the kids responded interestingly. Since I taught fourth grade, I had the same students all day, and of course I got to know them well. Most of my students had no experience with cats. They didn't dislike cats; they just didn't know any. Guard dogs were the pets of choice in the surrounding neighborhoods. A few students were actually afraid of the cat and didn't want him near them. It had never occurred to me that children might be afraid of cats. Fortunately, all but one child would eventually lose any fear of the cat over the school year.

So what did we name our classroom cat? We had a contest, but the outcome was unanimous. At home the kids were watching TV and seeing commercials for Frisky cat food. To my students, our classroom cat looked like the television cat, so his name became Frisky.

The kids were fascinated by Frisky, and it was clear to me that there was a lot better chance of learning in the classroom with the cat involved in my lesson plans. I integrated the curriculum with Frisky because he was such a motivational factor. For science lessons, we observed Frisky and his behaviors. We weighed and measured him. Kids were fascinated by watching his eyes dilate and change colors, and that was a good science lesson. We wrote poetry and stories about him. I would start them writing by saying things like, "What do you think Frisky did all weekend?" Or, "If Frisky could talk, what would he say?" I am still intrigued by the fact that before ADHD was called such in education, the kids who would have been diagnosed with that today were the ones most interested in the cat. The cat could hold their attention and help them focus.

When Frisky came to us we already had a gerbil in the room named Crooked Tail, named for obvious reasons. Crooked Tail lived in a twenty-dollar terrarium with some chicken wire over it held in place by heavy books. Frisky liked to sit on top of the tank and watch the gerbil, and the gerbil scooted right up against the glass to wiggle his nose and try to communicate with Frisky. Obviously Crooked Tail had no prior experiences with cats! I suspect watching the gerbil gave Frisky something to occupy his time at night, probably like watching kitty TV for him. Fortunately, Frisky never did anything predatory toward Crooked Tail.

Frisky enjoyed life in the classroom. He loved attention from all the kids. He rubbed on their legs throughout the day. He liked to perform a balancing act on the chalk rail during lessons, and in the process rub off whatever I'd written on the board with his hair. The kids loved that. Being a cat, of course, he spent much of his day sleeping—in the sun in the classroom's huge windows or in the open desks of the students. It was thrilling for a student to come to school in the morning and find Frisky in his or her desk. It felt very special to them.

Since I'd been warned to keep Frisky confined to the classroom, my students helped make sure he stayed put. Nevertheless, once in a while he would get out without anyone noticing, and over the intercom I would hear: "Mr. Peterson, there's a package for you in the office . . . again." I would retrieve the cat, and teachers would stick their heads out of their classrooms to chuckle as Frisky and I headed back to the classroom.

I enjoyed Frisky for myself, too. I'd never had a pet of my own. We often had a family pet when I was growing up, but none was mine alone, and none had been a cat. Now I had a cat of my own as soon as the school day was done. That's when Frisky gave me his full attention and wanted mine back. He acted like it was *his* time to be with me. He liked sitting on my desk and was good company while I worked. He wanted to play and be on my lap, and he would get upset when I left for the night. At first I took him home with me on the weekends, but eventually kids who had a note from their parents could take Frisky to their home for the weekend or for holidays. Parents would have to pick him up, of course, and I'd send his litter box and food home with them. There was never a problem while he was away. He was a very adaptable beast.

We had a good year with Frisky in the classroom. At the end of that school year, however, I decided to leave Flint to go to the Philippines with the Peace Corps. Before I left, there was a farewell party at school in which the kids and I celebrated our time together and hugged good-bye. When we talked about how Frisky had been such a cool cat, one little guy said to me, "You're the cool cat, Mr. Peterson."

Frisky and Crooked Tail moved to northern Michigan to live with my sister, and they lived good lives. Twenty years later, when I taught stateside again, I had another stray cat in the classroom named Blue. He was a cool cat, too, though my memories of Frisky are more vivid. I have always hoped that those experiences with Frisky and Blue in the classroom made my students more comfortable with cats during the rest of their lives. Not only did Frisky help make learning fun and accessible to the kids in the classrooms, I also felt he helped teach them how to know and care for other animals in the world. I know he did for me.

---

### Fight . . . or Freeze?

Even house cats can get a wild hair and do some damage on their humans if we're not careful. Is that tail starting to twitch from something you're doing? If you don't stop what's bugging kitty in time and kitty latches on to you with teeth and claws, don't fight it—instead, simply stop moving. Like many predators, cats need to see movement to get and stay excited. Remember, mama cat teaches her babies early on how to pounce so they can catch and eat meat. So freeze your movements, watch for kitty to relax, then swiftly withdraw. And, of course, keep the peroxide handy to treat whatever damage your mighty feline inflicts.

# The Mayor of Dreher Avenue

*Donna Hollingsworth with Pam Lione*

H e was born in the foundry off Dreher Avenue that had become part of the area's urban decay. His mother was a feral cat who managed to stay alive all the years I lived on the corner in an old duplex. My kids found him on a cold February night in the old trolley factory. The kids used to sneak over there, playing in the ruins of the dying landmark and getting home before I did so I wouldn't catch them there.

I had just moved in that December, and the heavy gray sky hovered over us like an ominous cloud. I was struggling in every way imaginable, consumed with guilt for my children having a single mom, one more choice that wasn't mine. I hated taking my children out of their home, and I was still reeling from the bank notice telling me our home was in foreclosure and that the house would be padlocked. I wondered how that could have happened without my knowledge. Our belongings were meager, so I packed what I could and moved my children into a part of town that would be another lesson in humility for all of us.

I had never before suffered from depression, but I could feel its pull threatening to overtake me, separating me from the rest of a world that seemed to be in color while I was living in black and white. In a way it was good that I was too tired to stop and think about my life. I was working three jobs: part time at a car dealership, selling Italian pastry at a flea market, and teaching ballet in the evenings. I was waiting for the court to decide child support while my three children acted out in ways I never imagined. I was most worried about my six-year-old daughter, Jill, who was often left in the care of her older brothers while I worked. They were angry and confused themselves, stepping in to fill their father's shoes.

It was Jill who convinced me to take the kitten. Her little hands had him in a choke hold, and her big, sad eyes pleaded with me. The kitten's small gray body hung suspended while his white-tipped paws batted at Jill.

"Please can we keep her?" We thought he was a girl then, not that I knew how to tell anyway. The vet would enlighten us later.

"No."

"Please!"

"No."

"*Pleeeease!*"

We went back and forth with me saying no and her saying please until I plucked him out of her hands before she choked him. He curled himself into a ball, exhausted from playing, and fit in the palm of my hand. I probably shouldn't have looked at him. He was beautiful, slate and white with eyes that softened my resolve. I did a mental sigh. *One more mouth to feed*, I thought, then added a litter box and kitty litter to the cost of food that would be required to keep him. At the time I didn't realize that this truly was a gift from above, one that would bless us for the rest of our lives.

We named him Kung Fu because when my oldest son, Tommy, played with him, the kitten would give him karate chops with his paws. He was so tiny in those first few weeks I was afraid we would crush him. We lost him once when we were going in and out of my back door with recital costumes for my ballet class. We searched the entire neighborhood and found him hours later, hiding under the stove, his little white paw poking out as if to play.

In the days that followed, this tiny ball of fur would elicit smiles and giggles from the children. He was still too young to realize that the piece of ribbon they were pulling away every time he tried to swipe it was attached to a child. As the days went by he grew wilder, and I was concerned he had somehow inherited his mother's feral ways. He would climb the side of the couch like a salamander, looking behind him to see if the children were chasing him.

One day I laughed out loud when I saw him jump from the lampshade he was suspended from, execute a triple-axel flip, and dismount on the couch, his four legs splayed underneath him. The kids looked up at me, as if the sound of my laughing was strange to them. I realized then that the atmosphere had changed in the house, that it had lightened somehow, and this scampering little monster was the reason. Late at night, after he had lay in my lap letting me absorb his warmth while he purred, he would go upstairs and curl up with one of the kids.

At first I thought he was a dog in a cat's body, as he would howl in protest when we left the house without him. It got to the point that I had to bring him to the studio where I was teaching ballet just to keep him quiet. There he would frolic with the little ballerinas. He would lie on his back and let them rub his tummy, and then he'd turn around and bite them.

He liked us to take him for a walk, and he would heel like a dog, keeping up the whole way. We lived on a busy street, and once, as I got out of my car after work, I saw Kung Fu sitting on the curb. I hurried toward him, horrified as I saw a car coming. At the sound of the car, the cat froze and pulled back. Then, as he sat on the curb, he looked one way, then the other, and scampered across the street to where the kids were. The three of them rushed to him, saying things like, "That's right, Kung Fu, look both ways!"

He was an odd animal, more human than cat. When I would make spaghetti sauce, he would sit by the stove and howl at the pot of simmering marinara, then jump up on the counter and lick what was left of the sauce off our plates. He did weird things, like give a high five if you raised your hand to him. He would do martial arts, carrying out a perfect karate chop, and sometimes he would nuzzle me and suck on my armpit. I fell in love with that furry little oddball, and in the strangest way he taught us all how to smile again, coming into our lives at a time when we needed him most.

Over the years Kung Fu would fight for his territory, and there were times we had to take him to the vet over lumps he took fighting with what were probably his brothers. He would bring me mice, proud to be keeping watch over the family home. He would charm the neighbors into feeding him, going door to door, getting treats and smiles. When he hit twenty-five pounds, blown up like a tick with arms and legs, I had to put him on a diet.

He grudgingly made room for Gunner, our German shepherd, and Emma, our pug. For the most part he would ignore Gunner, lifting his nose so as not to appear intimidated by the size of him, but he loved Emma. He would let her groom him, licking his face and neck. He'd bat his paws at Gunner when he tried to interfere. When we left Dreher Avenue, our neighbors were sorry to see Kung Fu go. They still talk about his oddball ways. Kung Fu is sixteen now, and a lot has changed in our lives. The kids are all grown. Tommy was injured in Iraq—a traumatic brain injury from an exploded mine. He came home different and yet the same. When he and his wife come to visit, Kung Fu curls up on his lap, not sitting with anyone else until Tommy goes home, sensing somehow that he's struggling. The kids have all grown up and moved on, and I managed to heal along the way, that dark time long behind me.

Kung Fu is still with me, an old man in a cat's body. He walks with me if I'm taking Emma for a walk. He still looks both ways before he crosses the street. He still eats spaghetti sauce every time I cook it. He still makes me smile when he lies down on his back and lets me rub his belly. And then he bites me.

# Kit Kat the Comforter

## Lonnie Hull DuPont

I love Christmas. I always have. I also love New Year's Day and then my birthday ten days later. Some adults dread the holidays, but not me. I've loved those holidays most of my life. This is not a Christmas story, but it is the story of one holiday season that could have gotten ugly had it not been for Kit Kat the Comforter.

Kit Kat is our handsome, husky tortoiseshell house cat. She lives with my husband, Joe, and me along with Lucy, our Russian Blue cat. Both cats were strays, each making her way to our door as a kitten, over a year apart. What profound good fortune was ours to have these beasts come to us and ask to move in.

As a feral youngster, Kit Kat handled herself well in the wild when we first saw her at around six months of age. She was vocal when hungry but otherwise skittish about being approached by humans, until she met Joe. She bonded with him when he fed her outdoors, and she allowed him to pet her.

After a couple months, Joe and I felt she would better survive the outdoors—where she seemed to want to be—if she were in a different setting. We lived on a state highway with lots of truck traffic, and we believed that taking her somewhere else could help this tough kitten survive. So one night we packed her up in a box and drove her to my sister's ranch eight miles away where the little cat could be a mouser in the barns. She was not happy about being boxed up and put in the car—she cried all the way there, and I cried all the way home. But we truly believed we were doing the right thing for her.

Ten nights later, I glanced out our front window and discovered a surprise. The little cat was back on our porch. She was watching the windows, waiting to be seen, and she was too tired to make a sound. Somehow she'd maneuvered eight country miles full of potential dangers to get back to us, avoiding coyotes and dogs, maneuvering her little self around a lake and farms and even across a busy highway. And now here she was—skinny, exhausted, hungry, and quiet. But apparently home at last. Joe and I decided right then that if this cat wanted to live with us that badly, she should. We opened the front door, and the skittish, feral kitten walked right in and stayed. We named her Kit Kat after that famous tail-twitching kitchen clock.

At first I thought Kit Kat was kind of odd-looking, but that's because I was not yet used to the unique beauty of a tortoise-shell cat. Mostly black with patches of cinnamon and honey, her unusual markings gave her an off-center look. Her upper eyelids were blond, as if she were wearing pale eye shadow to contrast with her dark fur. One dot of blonde fur on her face was placed so that it gave her a kind of feline beauty mark, a la Marilyn Monroe. Her eyes were round and hazel, her nose was black and slightly turned up. Once she moved in, it took only a short time for our skinny cat to fill out and become gorgeous. Of course Kit Kat had already bonded with Joe during her outdoor feedings. Now indoors, she waited for him to come home from work by facing the door she knew he would walk through. She would start that vigil at about five thirty. I was good enough for her when Joe was away, but once he came home, she watched him and followed him around like . . . well, you might say like a dog.

I accepted that Kit Kat would be Joe's cat. Then one day soon after Kit Kat moved indoors, I wasn't feeling well and decided to take a nap. Kit Kat joined me on the bed and curled up near my head as I dozed off. When I woke up, I was lying on my right side, and something was pressed against my right eye. I slowly opened my left eye and saw the profile of a black turned-up nose in my line of vision. Kit Kat's little head was tucked up against my right eye socket, and I could only see the silhouette of her nose. Maybe it was because that tough cat allowed herself to feel safe enough to sleep pressed against my face that made me fall in love with her right then. Her nuzzling up to me on a day when I didn't feel well was a sneak peek at things to come.

Joe and I both have strong personalities, but we became humbled by the reality that the strongest personality in our house was Kit Kat's. She is still with us as I write this, and how she gets us to do exactly what she wants continues to amaze us. How she refuses to do what she doesn't want to do is equally amazing. But what is most amazing of all is how this little strong-willed creature treats us when we aren't feeling quite up to par. We call her several nicknames: Kit Kat the Social Director (because she actually greets guests at the door), Kit Kat the Ferocious (because we've seen firsthand her expert hunting skills), and when we're not feeling well, she is Kit Kat the Comforter.

We first noticed her comforting skills when she had been with us just a couple of years. After the 9/11 tragedies, Joe's job required him to work extra hours to meet a related government-mandated deadline. His commute was over an hour each way, mostly on two-lane country roads, always in the dark. For a while he was coming home late every night. Sometimes he arrived home so exhausted that he would walk in the back door, head straight through the house to the bedroom, lie down with coat and shoes still on, and go immediately to sleep. After waiting so intently for Joe to come home, Kit Kat would follow him through the house, hop on the bed, and look him over, head to toe. Then she hunkered down next to him, leaning on his legs like a herding collie might, continuing to eye him. I would simply leave them alone so Joe could rest, since he clearly was in good paws.

As for me, I am prone to anxiety and have been since childhood. There are times when it sort of flares up, for lack of a better way to put it. When this happens and I'm home, Kit Kat suddenly appears from elsewhere in the house, jumps on my lap, and plasters her body across my chest, purring loudly over my heart. I don't know how a cat would know I am feeling anxious, but her behavior leads me to believe she does know. I imagine that if we took a blood pressure reading, mine goes down right then; certainly there's research that would support that. At any rate, once I feel calmer, my cat hops down and goes back to whatever she was doing.

Kit Kat also seems to be the Comforter-at-Large. One Thanksgiving week Joe and I were out of state with his family. I left a cat-sitter in charge of the beasts—a young college woman who unfortunately that very week was going through a bad breakup with her boyfriend. She called me every day during that trip to talk about it. On Thanksgiving Day, while everyone was waiting for me to join them at the table so they could start the big feast, my cat-sitter friend was sobbing uncontrollably on the phone. I finally told her, "Get Kit Kat and hold her and cry into her fur." That's exactly what she did, and Kit Kat purred all the way through it.

Joe and I had moved to my hometown to help with my aging parents, and in a matter of a few years, I lost my mother, my stepfather who raised me, my stepmother I lived with on weekends since I was five years old, my best friend from high school, and my current best friend—the two friends only in their forties. These deaths had their effect on me in many ways, but one of the biggest ways it showed was at Christmas. All of them liked Christmas, too.

My husband's family lives too far away for us to celebrate Christmas together very often, and we have no children. I have a few family members in the area, but still, at Christmastime, Joe and I celebrate much of it alone. Until recently, we did not have a church, and since we both work out of town, our sense of community can be rather fractured. We continue to look for ways to make holidays a special time, because that matters to me.

Two years ago I was especially enthusiastic about the upcoming holidays. I had worked very hard so that I could take time off work starting one week before Christmas and not return until after the New Year. I was so excited my first day off that I was like a little kid who doesn't know which fun thing to do first.

That lasted two days. Then I got hit hard with a sinus infection—something I had never had before. It left me literally sleepless for two weeks. Just as my round of antibiotics was finishing, I got a separate virus that kept me up coughing at night for four more weeks. For six weeks—through Christmas, New Year's, *and* my birthday—I was sick every single day. I constantly reminded myself that it was all temporary, just weird and unfortunate timing, but I felt like a little kid once again—this time, one who doesn't get to go to the party. Joe had to sleep in the living room most of that winter because of my coughing.

For all of her life with us, Kit Kat has slept with us. She hops up onto the end of the bed and walks up the middle between us to the head of the bed. Then she curls on her side like a little person, her head resting on her own small pillow between Joe's and my pillows. She stays warm and connected. Joe and I have been purred to sleep many a night and purred awake in the morning. Since Kit Kat has aged and occasionally suffers from joint pain, I bought her a carpeted pet stairway so she can get onto the bed easier. The day I brought it home, she watched me park it at the foot of the bed, then she marched right up the four steps to the top of the bed. No hesitation, no sniffing it over. She knew it was hers immediately, given to her so that she could continue to sleep with us.

But even though Kit Kat sleeps with the two of us, she favors Joe. So on the first night Joe slept in the living room because of my coughing, I shut the bedroom door, expecting Kit Kat would join Joe on the futon. Then I saw her black velvety paw reaching under the door. I got up and opened the door. Kit Kat sat back at the threshold and looked up at me. Then she looked over her shoulder toward the living room. She looked back up at me.

"Sorry, sweetie," I told her. "We're not together tonight. Do you want to come in?"

She did. As I lay back down, Kit Kat climbed up her stairs and onto the bed as usual and walked up the middle to her pillow.

But this time she did something different. She sat at her pillow and watched me. I lay down on my left side facing Kit Kat and immediately began coughing. She watched me for a bit, then she turned herself completely around so that she was facing the end of the bed. She hooked both her front paws over my arm and settled down like a camel. She kept her paws hooked over my arm while I coughed. Literally, she hung on to my arm. When I finished coughing, she leaned her face against me and went to sleep. She ignored her pillow. She did not sleep in the way she had slept for all the past ten years. Instead, she turned herself completely around and seemed to attend to me.

This went on most of the winter. Every night that Joe bunked on the futon, I got into bed and lay on my left side, and here came Kit Kat up the steps and up the middle of the bed. But she never slept curled on her side with her head on her pillow that winter; rather, she slept hunkered down on my arm. If I had a particularly tough coughing spell, she would wake up and hang on while I hacked away. If I turned over to my right side, she then turned on her left side, her purring body pressed against my back like a hot water bottle. And if I sat up for a while in the night because I couldn't breathe freely or I had to take medication, she sat up, too. We watched TV together sometimes most of the night until I could go back to sleep. Clearly we had a working cat that winter. She was my personal nurse. Joe said he envisioned her in a little old-fashioned blue cape and nurse's cap with a red cross on it.

I eventually started getting better, and one night Kit Kat slept with Joe in the living room instead of with me. That night my cough was controllable, and I slept good and hard. That first night I suspected the bad stuff was over and somehow Kit Kat knew it. She continued to sleep with Joe for the next couple nights, and I continued to get better until spring was on its way. Then we all slept in the same bed together again, Kit Kat curled on her side, her head back on her little pillow between Joe and me.

Since that strange and sickly winter, Kit Kat has not slept with me in the way she slept with me then—facing me, hanging on to my arm with her front legs. But I suspect if I need her comforting abilities in the future, she'll be right there, on duty.

# About a Boy

*Alison Hodgson*

B ooooooy! Boooooooy!" I called, standing at the very edge of the porch peering into the dark. It was not unusual for our cat to take an evening stroll, but it was raining and I was five months pregnant—exhausted—ready to turn in. I strained to hear the sound of him crashing through the shrubs and his friendly yowl that was his standard greeting. Nothing. This was the third time I had come down and called for him. I didn't like going to bed without Boy safely inside, but I assured myself he would be on the porch in the morning—indignant, but safe.

But he wasn't there in the morning. I called and called some more. Nothing. We needed to leave for work. Where could he be? He would be back when I returned, surely.

He wasn't.

I called the Humane Society. No cat matching Boy's description: male, large—enormous, really—long-haired Siamese with tiger markings on his belly. Since they didn't have anyone matching the minor distinctions, I didn't bother going into the major ones: his intelligence, vocal range, and great personality, engaged and engaging.

Boy's origin was the stuff of great literature: His mother, a seal point Himalayan (half Persian, half Siamese, with light brown fur and dark brown markings), a very fancy breed, fell on hard times and became a stray. My family lived in a clearing in the woods, and one day this raggedy little cat came walking up the drive. My sister, Torey, who was seven, took her in and named her Tess.

With a large wart on her head and a tail exposed at the end, the cartilage resembling a stick, Tessie was an unlikely heroine. She was a good, sweet girl, and—like many mothers in history— a mere conduit of greatness.

Right before her veterinary appointment to deal with the wart and the tail and to be spayed, she got out and mated with what we have to assume was a massive tiger cat.

The four kittens (two male, two female) were a gorgeous mix of both. One of the males and one of the females resembled Tess, but the male was big from the start, and as he grew, the distinct tiger stripes developed on his belly. Torey named them Girl and Boy respectively. The other male was big, like his brother, but silvery-gray, blue point Himalayan, and we appropriately named him Frosty. The other female was all black and named accurately (if inappropriately), Blackie.

"We are *not* keeping any of them," my father said.

My mother was picky about who took the kittens but quickly found homes for Girl, Frosty, and Blackie with family and friends long before they were ready to be parted from Tess.

In the meantime, Torey reveled in them. It was early summer, so they played together all day outside. I will never forget her running around the grass in the middle of our circle drive, long blond hair flying and shining in the sun, the kittens following in a single line, like something out of a storybook.

Once they were weaned, Torey had a little feeding ritual. She clacked the handles of the can opener together when she called them, and soon they knew that distinctive sound and came running. Eventually Torey only had to say, "Clank! Clank!" to summon the horde. Boy was the greediest and often had to be pulled away so his brother and sisters could have a chance.

All too soon they were old enough to go to their new homes, and one by one, Girl, Blackie, and finally Frosty left us. Only Boy remained.

"We're not keeping him," my father said.

My mother knew all she had to do was put a sign at the end of our drive, but she refused to give Boy away to a stranger. I don't know exactly how long it took—weeks, months, or a year—before Dad accepted what the rest of us had known all along: Boy wasn't going anywhere. By that time he knew his name, and we didn't try to change it.

Tessie was Torey's cat; Boy belonged to all of us. He loved to be held, like a babe in arms, his big belly exposed, his legs splayed. He happily joined us on walks, and when we called, he came. Somehow he was housebroken, though he preferred the great outdoors to the indignities of a litter box. Since there were six of us at home, there was always someone around to let him out.

He had a rich solitary life, too. Daily he rambled through our woods, happily roaming. He was a fierce hunter; rabbits were his favorite quarry. He was a country boy through and through.

For human males, never leaving home and over-closeness to one's mother is often fatal, but for Boy, it was his making. He was the most phlegmatic, expansive, and easygoing cat I've ever met. And he was the size of a small dog.

When I was in college, my parents sold the house in the woods. They rented a couple different houses after that, and each time Boy quickly adapted to his new circumstances. Finally, after all the kids were out of the house, my parents moved to an apartment that didn't allow animals.

My husband, Paul, and I, newly married, lived in an apartment in the city where cats were allowed. Paul was no fan of cats in general, but tolerant of Boy in particular, and he agreed to take him in. I promised to handle all his care.

Our landlords, an older couple, lived in the large apartment on the first floor and had two cats of their own, one of whom Boy promptly beat up when they met in the stairwell. My landlord came to tell me about it, and I couldn't believe it. Boy? My dear, precious Boy kitty? And yet I realized this was the classic response of the mother of a bully, and it occurred to me, outside of Tess, Boy had always ruled a one-cat fiefdom. I tried to keep him away from the landlords' cats.

With the exception of the litter box we were obliged to have him use, Boy took to city life with ease. He liked to stroll around the front yard while we sat on the porch. We were accustomed to his impressive size and somewhat inured to its wonders, but we were fairly often reminded. Once, a couple of college-age guys were walking by and saw Boy.

"Look at that Sasquatch!" one said to the other as they passed, staring. Paul and I beamed. *That* was a worthy sobriquet.

Paul and I were on the five-year plan, but I became pregnant soon after our first anniversary. Paul graciously took over Boy's litter and personal care, which was considerable. I was nervous about having a child so much sooner than we planned, but excited, too, and thankful that Boy would get to meet him or her. I had always known that when we had children someday, Boy would be safe for them to learn how to treat animals with dignity and respect.

There is no good time for your beloved cat to go missing, but being five months pregnant and in the middle of a weeklong rain has to be one of the worst.

I placed an ad in the paper, called the Humane Society every day, and walked door to door. Several neighbors I had never met knew Boy quite well.

"Oh, I love that cat!" one woman told me. "Every few days he shows up begging for food."

"Do you feed him?" I asked.

"I always give him a little something. He looks well fed, but he always seems so desperately hungry."

And that was just one house. I discovered he had a circuit he'd been working since he moved in with us. But no one had seen him for several days.

We lived in a three-story Victorian mansion with a corner tower, square on the first and round on the upper two stories. Our apartment was on the second floor, and the tower was an extension of our living room. Every night I stood, head pressed to the glass, weeping and praying, willing a small dark figure to cross the road and come into my sight.

There was only rain and darkness. I just couldn't believe this was how our story was going to end. I couldn't accept that I would never see him again, that I might never know what happened to my wonderful Boy.

The third morning I made my daily call to the Humane Society and gave his description: male, long-haired Siamese, and our street name: Cherry. "His name is Boy and he responds to the words *clank clank*."

"Just a second. Let me check."

I waited, clutching the phone, my ear pressed hard trying to hear anything. She got back on the line.

"When I said 'Boy' he looked up, and when I said 'Clank clank' he let out a big old meow. Lady, I think we've got your cat."

I started to cry.

At the Humane Society I happily paid a small fee and, clutching Boy to me, asked where he had been. They didn't know many of the details; an occupant of the large apartment building across the street from our house had called. I wanted to thank her and gave them my number.

She called soon after we got home. After we made it through my teary thanks and offers of rewards, her polite acceptance of the former and waving away any idea of the latter, we got down to piecing together the story. The very night Boy "disappeared," she found him roaming the hall outside her apartment. He was wet from the rain and seemed hungry. He would. Although she had two cats of her own, she took him in and fed him: an easy mark.

When I let him out that night—soon after a good dinner, mind you—he must have immediately headed across the street in search of prey. How he got into the building and up to the fifth floor was a mystery. I imagined him yowling imperiously at someone to open a door. But how did he make it up to her hall? Did he hop on the elevator? Slip up the stairs?

"He's a great cat. It was strange, he looked bedraggled, but I just knew he had to be someone's pet. He was so friendly and tame. All he wanted to do was sit on the radiator in my bathroom and look out the window. I felt terrible calling the Humane Society."

She believed she had let him down, which was ludicrous. I told her about his mooching around the neighborhood and how I cried myself to sleep three rainy nights and there he was just across the street, warm, dry and well-fed—of course—the entire time.

"Where do you live?" she asked.

"The big white Victorian on the corner of Cherry and Union. We're the apartment at the front of the second story. I'm standing in the tower looking up at your building right now."

"Just a second." I heard her walking. "I'm standing at the window in my bathroom, where your cat sat his entire visit, and I can see your apartment."

I waved.

"Yup, I see you."

What a Boy.

# Liar, Liar, Shades of Gray

*Cindy Crosby*

I always taught my kids to tell the truth. It took a cat to make a liar out of me.

We had moved from a subdivision to what we considered "the country": three acres with woods, extensive garden, and a creek. The backyard was perfect for baseball games and hide-and-seek for our two young children and their friends.

I was often called on to referee first base or solve small disputes. "Mom—she cheated!" "Mom—he didn't touch the base!" I would respond: "Are you telling the truth? Be honest." Not only did I insist on them telling the truth, I wanted it told straight. No shading it "just a little." I was inflexible.

Adjacent to our backyard ball field lived a young couple with a baby. They kept mostly to themselves. We saw them occasionally and waved, but they didn't seem inclined toward making friends. They had a white and tan cat, a scruffy-looking thing, that prowled around the woods behind our houses. We never saw them feed her. As country folks sometimes do, they let her fend for herself, eating mice and birds and whatever the woods might offer.

We nicknamed her "Mama Cat," as she was a prolific kitten producer. From time to time we'd see her and a few kittens scampering around the back acres. Varmints or diseases likely got the kittens, because we never saw them grow into cats. But sure as day follows night, more kittens took their place. Where suburban pet owners spayed and neutered, country folks let nature take its course.

One fall afternoon, our six-year-old daughter, Jenny, saw Mama Cat meowing piteously around our front door. "Mom, we've got to do something! Mama Cat's hungry!" I was slow to respond. We were currently in between cats, having put our seventeen-year-old calico to sleep the previous year. We had plenty of mouths to feed, however—a full-sized collie, an aquarium of tropical fish, and two zebra finches. We didn't need the responsibility of another cat.

I left the kitchen and followed Jenny to our front porch. *Meow.* What a scraggly ball of fur! And her dragging belly and engorged nipples were obvious signs of motherhood. *(Again! Oh, dear Lord.)* My heart softened. Together, Jenny and I raided the kitchen, then poured milk into a pan and emptied a can of tuna into a bowl. We took them to Mama Cat. She lunged for the tuna and licked the pan clean. Then she started on the milk. We left her on the porch, happily engaged.

Later that afternoon, I headed out the front door to the grocery store.

Uh-oh.

Mama Cat was tucked into the porch corner, close to the now empty bowls. Snuggled under her were five mewling kittens.

"Mom!" Jenny was right behind me. She bent over the kittens. "Five of them!"

Oh . . . were they cute.

"But look! They're cold!"

The kittens looked plenty warm to me, curled under their mama, but the concrete was surely none too comfortable.

My resolve weakened. I helped Jenny find a cardboard box that we lined with an old blanket, then we set it on the porch. Mama sniffed it; then, one by one, she moved the little ones in. Mama knew a good thing when she saw it.

I convinced myself we were just helping Mama Cat and her litter of little ones for a few days. We replenished the milk bowl as needed, and I bought more tuna. Soon I was buying cat food. A few days turned into a few weeks.

*Surely the neighbors will come and look for their cat,* I thought. I felt guilty. Were we taking over their pets? Finally I worked up my courage and went next door for a chat. Our neighbor laughed. She didn't seem worried. "That's fine—cats go where they want. She'll come back when she's ready."

I probably didn't mention the tuna.

Every day, when Jenny arrived home from school, her first stop was the kitten box. I'd often find her cross-legged, a kitten or two in her lap, reading stories out loud to a squirming audience. As the weeks passed, the kittens took on personalities and we gave them names. Our favorite was Jackie Blue, named for a song we liked by the Ozark Mountain Daredevils. Jackie Blue was scrappy and gray, with azure eyes.

The kittens grew. And grew. Mama Cat became bored with motherhood, frequently leaving the kittens alone to go off on prowls. I got impatient with our kitten situation. Kittens were underfoot when I walked out the front door. Kittens ran into the driveway when I pulled out of the garage. Kittens lurked in the shrubbery, flirted with the road out front. Disaster was surely just around the corner. It was time to find them homes.

I went back to the neighbors and told them the kittens were getting pretty big. Did they mind if we . . . "Nah, go ahead. . . . If you can find them homes, we're glad to see them settled." With this lukewarm endorsement, we tacked up the proverbial "Free Kittens" sign at the local veterinarian's office. We waited.

Who knew kittens would be so popular? The phone rang. And rang and rang. People showed up. A young couple came and left, cuddling a kitten. A family with small children picked out their favorite. Soon four kittens were gone . . . each with the promise of a good family and happy times ahead. Only one, Jackie Blue, remained with Mama Cat.

The box looked empty. "Hey, Jackie," Jenny told her. "You'll find a good home. Don't worry." Jackie snuggled into her arms and purred.

The phone rang again. I went to answer it.

"Do you still have the free kittens?" The woman's voice was harsh, abrupt.

"Well, yes . . ."

"I need a cat. Don't know if I want one, but I need one."

Great. She didn't exactly sound like a cat lover. "Well, we . . ."

"Stupid, lazy cats. Eat you out of house and home if you let them. But I've lost mine and I need to replace him. I've got mice. All over the house."

Okay, *not* a cat lover. "Listen, I don't know—"

She interrupted. "You got kittens or not?"

"Well, we've got one left." I said. It was the honest truth, but it choked me to say it.

"Me and my friend will be right over. Give us ten minutes."

I hung up and looked out the front door. Jenny was on the porch, reading *Meet Molly: An American Girl* to Jackie Blue, who was snoozing on her lap. Mama Cat was nowhere to be found.

I slowly went outside. "Honey, there are some people coming to see Jackie Blue."

Jenny looked up from the book and smiled. Jackie dozed on. "Did they sound nice?"

Huh. Always tell the truth. Right.

"No, honey, actually they didn't sound very nice. But it's hard to tell on the phone. They might be nicer than they sounded."

Her face clouded over. "Were they mean?"

I stalled for time. But I couldn't think of anything good to say. My expression said it for me.

"Mom—we wouldn't give Jackie Blue to a bad person, would we?"

"Well, no, but I told the lady we still had kittens. That was the truth . . ."

"Mom!" Her eyes welled with tears. "We can't give Jackie Blue to a bad person!"

I felt the same way. And the woman and her friend would be here any minute.

I made up my mind.

"Honey, take Jackie inside to your bedroom and close the door so she can't get out." Jenny's eyes widened. The kittens had never been allowed in the house. Scrabbling to her feet, she clutched Jackie Blue and went inside. Our collie met them at the door and followed them down the hall, barking excitedly. I heard the door close just as a battered sedan pulled into the driveway.

Oh, boy.

Out jumped a hard-looking brunette, followed by a frowzy blonde. The brunette strode up the driveway while I frantically thought. And thought. My mind was blank.

"You the woman with the kittens?" She spat out the sentence. I pasted a smile on my face.

"Well, yes, but . . ."

She folded her arms. They were big arms, muscular.

"Well, do you have one or don't you?"

I took a deep breath.

"I'm so sorry. We did have kittens, but we don't have any available now."

The woman's face folded up in a snarl. "What? I just called a few minutes ago! I thought you said you had one left!"

I tried to look sympathetic. "I know, I'm so sorry—we did have one left. But you came too late—we don't have any available anymore."

"Well, thanks for nothing." She and her friend whirled and stormed back to their car. They peeled down the driveway with a screech of tires.

I sat down on the front steps, close to the empty box, my heart hammering.

"Mom?"

It was Jenny. She had heard the whole conversation. "Are they gone?"

Unable to speak, I nodded my head.

"Did you lie to those ladies?"

"Well . . ." In a way, it was the truth. Our kitten wasn't available . . . to them.

I saw her struggle with this idea, rolling it around in her mind. Her face was puzzled.

I gave up. "Yes, honey. It wasn't really the truth."

Her face cleared and she grinned. "Lying is bad!" Then she hugged the kitten. "But I'm glad you didn't give them Jackie Blue."

It would be easier if choices were always black and white. But life is messy. Sometimes you have to weigh one wrong action against another. And sometimes, the truth is found in shades of gray.

A few days later we found a good home for Jackie Blue with a lovely, lonely widow. Jackie lived out the rest of her life pampered, well-fed, and the joy of her companion's heart.

Should I be sorry I shaded the truth?

Maybe not.

*How do I love thee?*
*Let me count the mice I kill*
*to drop at your feet.*

119

# A Different Kind of Cat

*Sandy Cathcart*

Smokey entered our lives in a ball of gray and white fur. He, like Domyeow and Si, was supposed to be a mouser—an outdoor cat to get rid of the varmints that terrorized our chickens and ducks. Smokey let us know right away that he was born for a different kind of duty, and years later I would be very glad he did.

I was pregnant with our fourth child when we brought Smokey home from the pound. Each of our three children sat in the backseat of our red Jeepster, taking turns holding Smokey in their laps, each trying to see who could make him purr the loudest.

"I've never heard a cat purr so loud," my husband, Charlie, remarked. I had to agree, and I also saw a problem arising—Smokey was already becoming a pet instead of the mouser we intended.

There are many rewards to raising children on a farm. They can run as carefree and wild as any animal, they enjoy spending more time in the outdoors than in front of a television, and

121

they learn firsthand about the cycle of nature and the gift of life. But there are also challenges for children on a farm, and one of the biggest is the need to differentiate between pets and working animals.

Unfortunately, our children (and often I) were unable to make that distinction. All of our animals became pets, and when it came time to butcher our first cow, the children and I cried for two days straight. Even Charlie decided not to butcher another rabbit after the first one traumatized our two oldest boys. We resorted to raising chickens and ducks for eggs, and milking our cow and goats.

So it wasn't that big a surprise when I found Smokey in bed with our oldest son on Smokey's first night on the farm. I tossed him from the bed, and to my surprise he landed with a thud on the floor—not on his feet like cats are known for. He was the only cat I've ever known who never learned to land on his feet.

The next morning, as soon as I lifted him, he began purring like a chainsaw. Holding him close to my chest, I rubbed his soft fur and felt a warm contentment wash over me. He smelled of pine and woodsmoke, and before I knew it, I was sitting in a chair enjoying the companionship only a cat can give instead of pursuing one of the many chores on my list.

That was one of the biggest gifts Smokey brought to my life . . . he was constantly reminding me to take a breather and enjoy a few moments of peace. For a young mother of three, trying to make a living off the land and living in a home with no electricity or running water, that was a special gift.

When my feet pumped the treadle sewing machine, Smokey would sit in the window seat watching and waiting until I had time to sit with him. When I snapped green beans, he would jump into my lap and watch the pieces fly into two separate bowls. When I was too engrossed in some project to give him attention, he would walk across the piano keys, making sinister music until I acknowledged his presence. When I worked in the garden, he walked beside me, pausing to munch on lettuce and other delectable greens. Smokey was a cat who loved vegetables and never ate any red meat—only tuna.

One day while I was washing dishes, Smokey lay in his favorite spot near the wood cookstove, soaking up the heat and watching my every move. When I stopped to fill his dish with food, Domyeow came through the door and plopped half a pack rat into Smokey's dish. I had read somewhere that such an act was meant as a supreme gift from one cat to another, but Smokey missed the significance. He jumped straight in the air backwards.

Domyeow never gave up trying to change Smokey's eating habits, often bringing him pieces of varmints she had captured, but to no avail. It was tuna and vegetables for Smokey and nothing else.

As far as contributing to farm life, Smokey was useless. He caught no varmints, ate no gophers, and didn't do a thing to earn his keep. According to most advisors I should have gotten rid of him immediately, but I never did. The reasons are many. That cat sat on my lap during cold winter evenings, keeping me warm and comforted with his soft purrs. During the summer months he would keep me company while Charlie was away working and the children were off on their own adventures. Still, I had no argument when well-meaning friends insisted he was useless—until Smokey did something that raised his status in our household forever.

It happened one cold November morning, four days before Thanksgiving. By now, our family had grown to five children. Nine-year-old Michelle was home sick from school, sharing an upstairs bedroom with five-year-old Clay and two-and-a-half-year-old Jocelyn, who were both supposed to be taking a nap. I was downstairs, dressed in a pair of my husband's sweat pants and old shirt, cleaning house. Happy noises from upstairs told me the children would not be sleeping today, but I hoped that at least the rest would help heal their small bodies. Then I heard the sound that every mother fears—the terror-filled cry of a child.

"Mama! Fire!"

I dropped the pan I was drying, grabbed a pail of water, and ran up the stairs two at a time. When I turned the corner, all air left my lungs. A box of clothes and a wall were on fire with flames reaching nearly to the ceiling! I threw the water over the flames and lifted Jocelyn from her crib. Then I placed her hand and Clay's hand in Michelle's and told them to head outside where they would be safe.

We had no phone to call for help, and Charlie had taken our only car to work. Our nearest neighbor was nearly a half mile away. We had 750 gallons of water in a tank next to the house, but the pipes were frozen. I had no way of getting the water out of the tank. I threw up a prayer to God for help and then turned back to try to tackle the fire.

I had seen movies where people had used blankets to smother a fire, so I grabbed a handmade quilt and dropped it over the flames. The fire disappeared and smoke dissipated, but just when I thought it had worked . . . Poof! The entire quilt burst into flame. I grabbed another and did the same, with the same results. After the third quilt burst into flame, I turned to head downstairs and nearly toppled Michelle backwards. All three children were still standing with their eyes opened wide, watching the flames.

"Out!" I shouted.

This time I lifted Jocelyn and pushed her siblings in front of me.

When they were a safe distance from the fire, I commanded them to stay put until I returned. Then I headed back into the house. Like most mothers, I had a plan for every emergency. In case of fire, I would get my children to safety and return for the photo and baby albums and my husband's paintings, but that's not what I did.

When I ran into the downstairs portion of our house, a strong sense of denial swept over me. There was no smoke downstairs and no flames. It all seemed so surreal. I turned in circles, wondering what to grab. Staring at my piano, a thousand memories flooded over me . . . my going through the first three piano lessons on a paper keyboard, my grandmother renting my first piano, and then finally my parents buying me this piano. The piano that traveled around the country with me until the day Charlie built the walls around the piano and said he would never move it again. All at once, everything seemed important.

Like a boat with one oar, I kept turning circles, unable to register the danger of my situation, until a flash of gray and white streaked across the room and grabbed my full attention.

It was Smokey, frantically looking for a way out.

Suddenly I knew what to do.

I ran for Smokey and lifted the frightened cat in my arms, then grabbed my purse and guitar on the way out of the house. When I sat Smokey on the ground, he ran off as if a monster were at his heels. I sat my purse and guitar on the ground and turned to go back into the house for the photo and baby albums. As I turned, Michelle screamed, "Mama!" and my eyes lifted to the upstairs floor.

Flames were reaching high into the sky, and the upstairs windows had melted. I realized in that moment that the upstairs floor would soon be crashing into the floor below. If it hadn't been for Smokey, I would have been caught in those flames.

We lost all our worldly belongings that day, and with less than ten dollars in the bank and no insurance, we found ourselves homeless for the next five months. But because of a cat named Smokey, a cat that most friends said was useless, not one of our lives was lost. Through that experience we discovered that real treasures are not bound in the things we own, but in the people and animals we love.

A verse in 1 Corinthians 1 says that God chose the weak things of the world to shame the wise. I believe Smokey, my little vegetable-loving cat who didn't even know how to land on his feet, was one of those weak and foolish things that God used in a big way. And I'm so glad He did.

# Lost in Translation

*April McGowan*

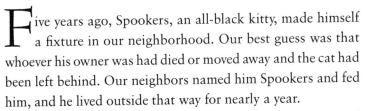

Five years ago, Spookers, an all-black kitty, made himself a fixture in our neighborhood. Our best guess was that whoever his owner was had died or moved away and the cat had been left behind. Our neighbors named him Spookers and fed him, and he lived outside that way for nearly a year.

Spookers had a habit of greeting anyone in the neighborhood as soon as he or she stepped outside the front door. He was just so happy to see . . . anyone. He'd meow and call, and we'd call back. We'd hear him long before we saw him. My children turned it into a game, to see who could spot him first. Sometimes he'd come out of some bushes, but more often than not he'd climb down from the wheel well of a car and saunter over to greet us. He'd wrap himself around our legs and purr.

Oftentimes, when we'd pull out in our car, I'd keep my eye on the rearview mirror as Spookers went and sat in the middle of the road, watching us drive away. Our side street isn't very busy, but the connecting roads are wild. The kids and I worried about his well-being, but my husband, Ken, had put his foot down months before. No more pets!

Once, our neighbors went on vacation for a week and asked us to feed their indoor kitties and Spookers while they were gone. We were glad to help. As we approached Spookers with the food can and changed his water, my young son reached out to pet him. Spookers shied away, and I wondered if he wasn't used to small children. I don't know what made me do it, but I started to talk to him as if he understood.

"Spookers, Seth would like to pet you. Would that be okay?"

Spookers looked at my daughter, Madeline, then at my son, and proceeded to walk right up to Seth and sit still while my three-year-old petted him. Seth was thrilled. My daughter and I laughed—it was as if Spookers understood us perfectly. This wouldn't be the last time we'd swear he understood English.

Over time, even though he was well fed, Spookers began to look sickly. He had sores showing up through his fur, and he was limping. My heart ached for him—he was such a sweet kitty. Sometimes I'd sneak him some lunch meat or a bit of tuna, but I did my best to honor my husband's wishes. We'd just buried our bird of fifteen years, our rats of three years, and found a home for our fish. We were pet-free for the first time in our marriage, and my husband wanted it to stay that way. I respected that—trust me, I'd had enough of cleaning cages to last me a lifetime. To top it off, I suffered from allergies—cats included. Adopting a cat would be a bad idea.

We live in the Pacific Northwest, a temperate area—but that Christmastime the temperature dropped to a frigid eighteen degrees. I grew worried about our little fuzzy friend. Spookers still met us outside every time we left the house, but his limping was much worse, and the sores on his body made it impossible for us to pet him anywhere but the top of his head. Still, he greeted us happily as if all was well with the world.

That night I approached the neighbors and asked if they'd be taking him inside, as the temperature was supposed to go even lower. They responded that they'd made him a place to hide—a plastic bin with a door cut out and pillow tucked inside made a cozy home in most weather. But I feared this wouldn't protect him from freezing. I kept picturing him all alone, falling asleep and never waking up again. I wanted to take him home and make sure he'd be safe, but it just didn't seem possible.

I talked to Ken about bringing Spookers home. He reminded me that I'd been talking about getting a dog one day. I wasn't allergic to dogs. I tried convincing him I'd be careful—not letting Spookers on the bed, keeping the house extra clean—rationalizing my allergies away. Ken, having raised several cats during childhood, rolled his eyes at me. You couldn't contain a cat like that.

That night I cooked Spookers dinner, in hopes the warm hamburger would help stave off the cold. Ken, a tenderhearted man, built him another box on our porch and said if Spookers was still there in the morning, we'd probably keep him. The kids' hopes rose. To my knowledge, Spookers had never slept on our porch, and there really wasn't a reason for him to do so that night. But I coaxed him over and gave him the hamburger.

I talked with him while he ate. "Spookers, if you stay here tonight, then we'll probably keep you." I gave him a pat on the head. He gave me a long, lingering look with his big green eyes before settling stiffly into his makeshift bed.

When I went back inside, I expressed my worry to Ken, and he said he'd check on him during the night. If he thought Spookers was in any danger, he'd bring him in the garage. At 1:00 a.m. I heard the front door opening and my husband murmuring soft words. I knew I'd find Spookers in the garage in the morning. Spookers had chosen to take my advice and stay on the porch.

The next morning my husband gave in to the longing looks that the kids and I gave him. After making us promise that he'd never have to clean any cat boxes—ever—he said we could keep Spookers as long as I didn't have a reaction to him.

We checked with the neighbors to make sure they didn't have any lingering feelings for Spookers, and they assured me of their relief that someone was taking him in. Then we headed to the vet to see what might be wrong with our furry pal. The vet informed us Spookers wasn't a very old kitty, maybe five, but he had a bad case of arthritis in his knees. And the sores and runny nose were from seasonal allergies plus car oil and fluids dripping on him from sleeping in the wheel wells. As soon as I heard he had allergies, too, I started to laugh. What could be more perfect? The vet gave him his shots and sent us on our way with our new kitty.

After inspecting his new food dishes and litter box and giving a cursory look around his new digs, Spookers promptly climbed up into my husband's lap for a nap. I think he knew who he had to work on first.

Days merged into weeks, and all the sores on Spookers's body healed. He began to put on weight, and within the month, he had the look of a shiny, healthy cat. When we invited the neighbors over to see him, they could hardly believe it was Spookers. With the exception of a runny nose if he sat next to an open window (allergies, remember?), he was like a brand-new kitty.

And what about *my* allergies? Strangely enough, even though other people's cats set off my eyes and asthma, Spookers doesn't bother me in the least.

I've never had a cat before, but my husband assures me he's never known one like Spookers. Spookers has the best temperament of any cat he's ever seen. Not only is he easygoing and slow to anger, but Spookers comes when called. He also knows *our* names.

One day, while we were sitting in the bedroom, the cat between my husband and me on the bed (yes . . . the bed), my husband asked me where our son was. I mentioned Seth was in the bathroom, and Spookers turned and looked at the bathroom door. My husband laughed and said, "Where's Mom?" and Spookers turned and looked at me.

I asked, "Where's Madeline?" and Spookers turned toward the direction of my daughter's bedroom. We went back and forth, each time getting the correct responses from him—too often to be just coincidence. A few months later, when we took in a second abandoned kitty (much to Ken's chagrin and our promises never to do it again) and this cat didn't even look our direction when we spoke to him, I realized how special Spookers's ability really was.

Five years later, I can't imagine what our household would be like without our furry black shadow. After my suffering from chronic illness for the past couple years, I'm feeling more and more blessed by his presence. Spookers seems to sense when I need comfort. He loves to nap with me, and he protests loudly if I won't follow him down the hall at bedtime. He's very chatty, telling us how much he misses us when we're gone. Or when he's out of food. Or, heaven forbid, if his litter box is dirty. And sometimes he just comes and sits by me and talks. I often wish I knew what *he* was saying!

I'm so thankful we took in that sore-ridden, helpless waif. He has blessed us more times than I can mention with his devotion and love.

## The Cat in the Box

We cat guardians have an unwritten contract with our house cats, and it goes something like this:

> I, your human, will do anything you want (within reason) to facilitate a good life for you. This includes:
> providing safety, warmth, and cool toys;
> feeding you when and what you like;
> giving affection (only when you want, of course);
> dispensing catnip on occasion;
> offering high places for indulging your sense of superiority and low places for hiding when I want to find you;
> and keeping the litter box clean.
> In return, you, my cat, will eliminate in that box and only in that box, and nowhere else.

That's all we ask, isn't it? How can we help make it happen? Cats get anxious when there's not a clean box to use and enough clean litter to bury things properly. We don't like the litter box to stink, and cats don't like it to stink, either. They have far more powerful olfactory senses than we have, and strong personal odors can be overpowering for cats and even feel threatening. This goes back to predator behavior. Plus, in multiple-cat homes, the box is often the setting for territorial showdowns. It's a big deal, that box. So help a kitty out:

1. Have one more litter box than you have cats. If you simply cannot do that, at least provide one box per number of cats.
2. Put boxes in private areas. And guess what—cats usually don't like the laundry room for their litter-box experience. It's noisy and has strong fragrances. If you absolutely must use that room, make sure the sound and vibrations of the machines aren't too close to the box. And keep scented laundry products off the floor—to a cat's nose, those scents (especially anything citrus) are distracting.
3. Scoop daily and change litter weekly.
4. Don't switch litter brands if you can help it. If your brand suddenly disappears from the shelves, use what you have remaining mixed with the new stuff so that there's a gradual shift.

# On a Farm

*Andrea Doering*

For the first six years of their lives, my children's favorite book was a slim Golden Books paperback titled *The Farm Book*. Every night—and sometimes during the day—we read through a day on the farm, vicariously meeting and caring for all the farm animals on those brightly colored pages. My husband, Ron, and I are not farmers, or even campers; our days are spent shuttling on trains and subways around the NYC area.

So one summer I decided it was time to see real-life versions of those animals, so we booked a stay at a working dairy farm in upstate New York. I was particularly happy with this choice for our son, Henry. Like many boys, Henry was always in motion and always touching the world around him. It wasn't enough to see it—he wanted to hold it, manipulate it, see what the world could do.

Henry, at five, easily taxed the capacity of our house and yard to fill his needs. And though we went to the park and beach as much as we could, there never seemed to be enough room to roam.

I was constantly in search of vast stretches of earth for him to ramble and explore, with lots of things to pick up and toss and take apart without hitting someone or damaging property. *This trip will be great,* I thought. An entire farm with cows to milk, horses to feed, a huge yard, a pond to fish in, and acres and acres to work with. *He'll be able to run around and completely wear himself out!*

We arrived at the farm in the afternoon, met our hosts, and took a brief tour of the buildings and animals. Sure enough, there were the horses and cows and goats and chickens, and I patted myself on the back with one hand and gave myself a "Blue Ribbon Mom" medal with the other. I gave the kids permission to explore while I unpacked in our cottage and enjoyed a few minutes of farm life. (Now would be a good time to tell you that I never tired of reading *The Farm Book.*)

Dinner was a communal event at the farmhouse, and our hosts had warned us—on a farm you come when the bell rings, because life is too busy to stop and make meals for people at all hours. So when the dinner bell rang, I went in search of three children, who seemed to have disappeared. They were not in the barn, not by the tire swing, not by the horses or chicken coop. I entered the back door of the farmhouse with a puzzled look on my face. I popped into the kitchen where our hosts were busy dishing up dinner, and before I even got the question out, the farmer's wife nodded her

head toward the front porch. "We have a new litter of kittens. If you're ever looking for your children, just go to the front porch."

134

Sure enough—there were my three little ones, snuggled side by side on a porch swing with eight kittens tucked into every crevice around and between them. And so quiet! They passed kittens back and forth, noting their eyes and color and personalities. It was a reluctant trio I moved into the dining room that day, and only the promise that they could come right back after dinner made the idea of leaving possible.

We spent four days at the farm. The girls began and ended their days with the kittens, and eagerly rambled through the rest of farm life in between. Emily, just six years old, bossed those cows around like she was born to it. Katherine was a part of it all—haying, milking, and especially looking at horses. But Henry never left the front yard. At this moment in his life he was determined to wear his blue rain boots every day, regardless of the weather. It was quite a sight to see him pop up out of bed, put on his Wellies, grab a Pop-Tart (we were on vacation, after all), and head across the field toward the generous front porch of a white clapboard farmhouse, his bright blond head shining in the sunlight.

And so this child I had endeavored to find acres of room for happily contented himself with a small patch of grass, beautifully shaded by trees, with just a few elements—a hammock, a porch swing, and a few worn farmhouse steps. And, of course, a cardboard box with eight farm kittens. All my photos of Henry from that trip show him and a kitten or two or three, lazing in the hammock, lying on the grass, staring at each other or the blue sky. And though it wasn't the vacation I had envisioned for him, it was the one he needed. No one told him to stop touching, stop running, stop anything. The kittens were the perfect companions for him, and I believe he found some kindred spirits among them.

Watching Henry on the farm made me think about how we use motion and speech to get noticed in a world that is far too busy, far too loud. But with a kitten, on a farm, you are noticed. You are valued for your sheer existence, and there is no need to talk or move. It's enough to sit in a hammock in your blue Wellies and be available as a soft landing place for a small creature.

Today I'm finishing this piece after picking up the now six-foot teenage Henry from lacrosse practice. He still loves to move fast and touch the world around him. But animals continue to flock to Henry, who, in their presence, becomes still and quiet. He is noticed and known among them—and is at rest.

# Blossom

*Marilyn Guidinger*

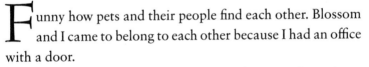

Funny how pets and their people find each other. Blossom and I came to belong to each other because I had an office with a door.

I worked in a big open laboratory with a very few private offices for the managers. One morning one of the technicians asked me if I would keep a kitten in my office for her. On her way to work she had rescued this orange kitten that was crouched in the middle of a busy traffic intersection. My co-worker couldn't take the kitten home until the workday was over, and she needed a confined place for it. My office fit the bill.

The kitten sat on my visitor's chair next to my desk. She had round cheeks and blue eyes, was sweet and friendly, and gave a meow occasionally to keep in touch while I worked. When I was on the phone, she'd jump from her chair and onto my back, clinging to me with her claws to let me know she didn't appreciate my not paying attention to her.

The technician who found the kitten wanted to keep her, so she took her home that night. Unfortunately for the tech, her landlord would not allow pets, so she brought the cat back to work the next day and asked me to cat-sit for another day while she found a home for the kitten. I endured another day of the cat hurling herself at my back and hanging on with her claws. She would look at me with bright, friendly eyes that said, "You are wonderful, please keep me!" She was a talker and meowed conversationally on a regular basis. Claws aside, by the end of the day, I was smitten. No one at work wanted the cat (except me), so I took her home to my two boys.

I grew up on a farm, and of course we had lots of cats to keep the mouse population under control, so I was a cat person from day one. Every spring there would be baby kittens to care for and enjoy. After the kittens were born, we'd look for the nest where mama cat hid them, sometimes in the hayloft of the barn.

The little kittens, their eyes not yet open, would instinctively hiss at us when we picked them up. Sometimes the kittens would get an infection in their eyes for which we had an antibacterial ointment from the veterinarian. If mama cat didn't like all the attention her kittens were getting, she would move them by carefully picking them up in her mouth by the scruff of the neck and carrying then to a new hiding place.

Once or twice something would happen to mama cat and we would have to bring the kittens into the house and feed them milk with a doll's nursing bottle. We kept them in a wicker basket lined with a towel until they got big enough to run around, then they were put on the back porch. After I left home for college and married life, I didn't have any pets until my own children were big enough to care for cats properly.

I wanted my two boys to experience caring for and being responsible for a pet. One day, after noticing an ad in the paper, I took the boys for a surprise ride in the car. We went to a home where kittens were being given away, and each boy got to choose his kitten. The boys couldn't believe it! They had wanted pets, but I had always said no, emphasizing the care a pet requires. Chris picked up a kitten who proceeded to lick his face. She was christened "Licky" and adopted as Chris's cat. Bob chose a tortoiseshell cat with a black mask on her face and dubbed her "Masky." Cats in hand, we drove home, and the adventure began.

Because I had such fond memories of raising kittens, we decided to let the two cats have one litter of kittens each before spaying Licky and Masky. Masky's kittens were born in the middle of the night. I awoke around 3:00 a.m. to hear high-pitched little mews coming from the family room. "They're here!" I told the boys, and we gathered around the tiny creatures. Licky's kittens followed two weeks later.

We had several generations of cats at home and assigned a cat from each generation to each of the boys, who then had the responsibility to care for that cat. About this time, my husband and I were no longer together. The boys divided their time between parents, and the cats went to their father's house.

Now, after acquiring this kitten from work, I announced to my boys that I had brought home a cat for myself. They couldn't believe their mom was actually going to have a pet of her own. I needed a name for the cat, and because she was a soft, orange puff of a cat, I named her Orange Blossom, or Blossom for short. Years later my younger son said he was so glad I had Blossom at a very lonely time in my life, and that Blossom and I seemed to love and have loyalty to each other.

Blossom loved to ride in the car. But even though she was cat-box trained, the minute the car started moving, she would urinate. Not to worry. We simply put a cat box in the car, which she used faithfully. She liked to ride sitting up straight on my shoulder so she could watch where we were going.

Blossom's favorite food was cantaloupe. If she saw me cutting one up, she'd look up at me and I'd get a sweet meow that said, "Remember what a wonderful cat I am, and you are wonderful, too, especially if you give me some cantaloupe." Watermelon or honeydew would do in a pinch.

It was twenty-five years ago that Blossom lived with us. Just thinking of her brings me joy. As I was writing this story of Blossom, I emailed my two sons to see what they remembered about her. Despite the fact that I often wait days for a response from them, they both wrote back immediately about her. She lovingly lives on in our memories.

# An Uncanny Cat Story

## Melody Carlson

One summer evening in Springfield, Oregon, a long time ago, a crazed-looking black-and-white kitten showed up at our kitchen door and started clawing furiously on the glass. Because we lived in a rural area with not many neighbors nearby, we were curious about the origins of this strange little feline. Why was it so intent on getting into our house?

My husband, Chris, opened the door, and the frantic kitten barreled in. Running in circles and bumping into walls and spinning about, it was obvious this creature was traumatized by something. Even when our young pet-loving sons, Gabe and Luke, tried to soothe the kitty, it was like an over-wound mechanical toy, unable to stop moving. I began to suspect the poor animal had been poisoned or drugged. After a while we enticed it to drink some milk, and it eventually settled down and fell into a deep sleep.

By the next day our boys had both fallen in love with our unexpected feline guest, and the previous night's crazy cat was replaced by a sweetly calm and loving kitty. Never mind that we didn't need another pet—we already had a re-homed terrier named Prince and a big yellow cat named Homer who'd adopted us. But Luke claimed the kitty as his own and named him Peppermint. He said it was because the cat's black-and-white stripes swirled around like peppermint drops. I immediately shortened his name to Pepper, because he'd been so peppy when we met him. Since we lived in the country, I assumed someone had dropped him off to find a good home—and it seemed he definitely had one now.

A couple days later I walked to my nearest neighbor's house to pick up some cucumbers and tomatoes that she wanted to share from her garden. Carla and I had just finished filling a bag when I noticed her son, Morgan, approaching us with a big grin. In his arms was a very familiar-looking black-and-white kitten. Had Pepper followed me over here?

"Hey, Morgan, it looks like you found our new kitten." I reached out for Pepper, thinking I'd carry him back home.

"That's *our* kitten," Carla abruptly informed me.

"Really?" I gave her a doubtful frown and was about to ask why this cat had been eating and sleeping at our house the past few days if he really belonged to them.

"We got him last weekend from my mom," Carla explained.

Dumbfounded, I petted the kitten's head, thanked Carla for the vegetables, and headed for home. Hopefully I'd come up with a gentle way to break the unfortunate news to my boys that Pepper really belonged to the neighbors. But while putting away my produce, I felt thoroughly perplexed. Something about this kitty situation was fishy—and it wasn't just the cat food we'd been feeding little Pepper. Was it really possible that this cat had two homes?

When I discovered Luke playing with the kitty in our back-yard, I felt even more perplexed. Had Pepper followed me back home earlier? And if so, maybe he was making it clear that he wanted to live here.

"Come with me," I told Luke. "And bring Pepper with you." As we walked through the field that led to the neighbors' house, I explained that there might be some confusion regarding the kitty's ownership. I was trying to prepare Luke for the worst, but at the same time I was reassured that since our neighbor Morgan was also Luke's best friend, we should be able to resolve this kitty dilemma amicably. Perhaps joint custody.

When we reached our neighbors' backyard, I was glad to see that Morgan was still outside, but I was stunned to see that he was playing with his black-and-white kitten—a cat that looked almost identical to ours. Naturally, Luke and Morgan compared their new pets with typical boyish amusement, and they thought it was funny that I couldn't tell the two cats apart.

"Our cat has more stripes than yours," Luke proclaimed.

"But our cat has this great white spot on his chest," Morgan pointed out.

"See why I was confused," I told Carla as she joined us. "Our kitten looks just like yours."

"You're right," she agreed. "How odd."

Morgan and Luke put the felines down in the grass, and the kitties were attracted to each other like magnets. Soon they were tumbling and tussling like a pair of old buddies—as if they'd already met. We all watched with fascination as I explained the bizarre way our kitten had shown up on Sunday night.

"Do you think they're related?" I asked Carla.

"No," she told me. "Not unless you've been to Portland. We got our kitty when we stayed at my mom's house last weekend."

"What's your cat's name?" Luke asked Morgan.

"Salt," Morgan proclaimed.

Luke burst out laughing. "*Salt?* My kitty's name is *Pepper.*"

"*Salt and Pepper?*" Carla and I said almost simultaneously.

"Why'd you name him Salt?" Luke asked his pal.

"Because it looks like he spilled salt down his chest," Morgan told him. They both just laughed harder. But I was thinking this was getting weirder and weirder.

"Are you sure these cats aren't related?" I questioned Carla. "Is it possible you brought home two cats by mistake?"

"No, of course, not," she assured me. "We would've noticed a second cat."

"Maybe Pepper slipped underneath your car somewhere, or up in the engine," I tried. "We had a cat that used to climb into the motor area in the wintertime because it was warm in there."

"It's summer," she reminded me. I could tell her patience with my theories was wearing thin.

"But if Pepper rode in the engine, it might explain why he was so traumatized when he showed up on Sunday night."

She seemed to consider this. "But it's a *two-hour* drive on the freeway." She firmly shook her head. "Impossible."

As Luke and I happily took our kitten home, I wasn't completely convinced it was impossible. First of all there was the timing—Pepper had shown up the same day the neighbors came home. Plus there was the odd way Pepper acted—like he'd been through an ordeal. Then there was how the kittens looked alike and bonded so instantly. It was all very uncanny. In my mind, those two cats were brothers. And if Pepper could talk, I'm sure he would have confessed to having stowed away in the neighbor's station wagon in order to remain with his brother. Because, obviously, Salt and Pepper belonged together.

# The Subway Kitten

## *Kathi Lipp*

Be careful what you say out loud.

When my husband was going to college, long before we met, he told God, "I will go anywhere you want me to go. Except California. That's the only place I don't want to live. The people there are weird and I just don't want to go there."

Well, if Roger and I have learned anything from that prayer, we sure are glad that God doesn't always take our ultimatums. That was twenty-five years ago, and Roger has been making his home happily in California ever since. So while I knew that Roger would follow God wherever He took him, he was a little less flexible with me and my wants and desires.

Roger had instituted a "No New Pets" policy in our home. We already had one cat and one dog. So even though I tried to convince my husband that our dog was lonely and needed another friend, and a kitten would keep our older cat young and feisty, Roger was firm. "No New Pets."

You see, like most couples, my husband and I lead very hectic lives. Roger works full time at a large technology firm about an hour away from our home in Silicon Valley, in addition to managing much of our ministry of writing and speaking. I'm on airplanes so often for speaking engagements that I've qualified for several status upgrades on airline frequent-flyer plans. With the amount of traveling we do, and how much it costs to have our dog boarded or our cat "sat," it didn't make sense to bring another animal into our brood. Except to me.

"*Please*, Roger. I just feel like we need a third," I would cry.

"No. Kathi, I love you, but another animal will tip me over the edge." I had to respect my husband's wishes. After all, before we were married, the only thing Roger had close to a pet was a goldfish—and his goldfish was made out of glass. "See! The perfect pet! He can take care of himself."

With our usually packed schedules, we were shocked to find ourselves one Saturday morning without places to go or people to see. We were both excited to have a day to relax and take it easy. No agenda, no pressure, nothing but an unplanned day stretching out in front of us.

We set out for our morning stroll with our puggle, Jake. Jake normally gets a quick walk in the morning since we're usually off to work or some appointment, but this day we decided to take a longer walk just to get the blood pumping and to give Jake some leisurely sniffing opportunities.

At the farthest point in our walk, I had a second wind. "Hey, Rog, would you like to take the long way? We don't have anything we have to do today. And Jakey would love it."

Roger stopped and considered for a moment, and said, "Sure, why not."

We started down the path that would take us behind the church property near our home when not twenty seconds later Roger said, "Is that a squirrel or a kitten?"

I looked to where Roger was pointing and saw a piece of gray fuzz no bigger than a deck of cards standing to the right of the walking path. It was a tiny kitten.

It was obvious that this kitten had been through a lot. Its eyes were closed and covered over with gook. Its breathing was labored and sounded wet and raspy. And it was obvious that whoever it was supposed to be with was no longer around.

I instantly scooped up the charcoal fur baby. I knew from prior experience that a kitten by itself shouldn't be picked up—Mom may be nearby. However, it quickly became apparent that if someone didn't intervene, this kitten was not long for this world.

Two hours at the vet and we received a very bad prognosis and a new piece of information: We had a girl! This little piece of fuzz weighing in at a whopping seven ounces was a baby girl. But our excitement was tempered with the vet's words: "Don't get attached. All you're going to be able to do is make her comfortable . . ."

So with several hundred dollars of medicine in my purse (the vet was kind enough to waive the examination fee, seeing as we were trying to be the animal kingdom's version of the Good Samaritan), we set off for home to wait, pray, and medicate.

We gave her the name Ashley. My son, Justen, wanted to give her a name that she could live up to. "It's for Ashes, like the Phoenix rising from the ashes. Ashley," he said. I thought he was being optimistic about her prognosis, but I wasn't going to be the one to squelch his hope. So we dubbed her Ashley.

For three days Roger and I took turns holding Ashley, giving her the medicine that she hated, and feeding her with a bottle that resembled the ones my daughter used to give to her baby dolls. At the end of those three days we had to face the facts:

Ashley wasn't eating. She seemed to spit up as much formula as we got down her, and she wasn't gaining weight.

And Roger was devastated. He couldn't hold her on that third day without tears welling up in his eyes. As much as he didn't want another cat, he had come to love this one and didn't want to lose her.

On that third day we needed a break. We were both sleep-deprived, cranky, and sad. So Roger ran out to get us lunch while Ashley and I took a nap on the couch. When Roger got back, his first question was, "Did she eat anything?" And I had to tell him no, she hadn't touched her food and had spit up her milk. Again.

We were tired, we were defeated, and we were hungry. I knew that Roger sensed I needed a boost, so instead of my normal low-cal order from Subway, he brought me my favorite: a tuna salad on honey wheat bread. I was so hungry, I ripped into the sandwich while still holding Ashley on my chest. But apparently, I wasn't the only one who had found her appetite.

Deep inside Ashley, some kitty instinct kicked into gear. As soon as Ash smelled that tuna, she was all over me—and my sandwich.

I scooped a fingernail full of tuna off the roll and offered it to Ash. She devoured it like the starving kitty she was. After that, I got her the tuna-flavored kitten food we had offered her so many times before. This time she ate it with gusto.

And now, several months later, after overcoming an upper respiratory infection, two eye infections, and an ear infection, we have Ashley Jared. Ashley, for that Phoenix rising from the ashes, and Jared, named after the spokesman for Subway sandwiches—the sandwiches that gave us back the kitten we didn't know we wanted in the first place.

Roger, who wanted nothing to do with cats, now has two.

# Fetching Ez

### *David Manuel*

I hated cats. I was a dog person through and through. With a dog, you always know what they're thinking, and once they're yours, they would rather starve than leave your side. They love you and make no bones about it. You want them to be affectionate? They are *there*.

Cats, on the other hand, are totally self-absorbed and wholly unpredictable. You might think they love you, but don't ever forget to feed them. . . . As for showing affection, if they do at all, it is strictly on their terms, and usually when it is most inconvenient. If you are focused on your computer, a cat will come and sit on the keyboard and not move until it has your undivided attention.

Conversely, if you are watching TV and wouldn't mind if a cat wanted to curl up in your lap, that's the *last* place it would choose—unless, of course, you are reading a book and would rather not have the cat in your lap. Then that's the *only* place it wants to be. And in the morning the cat decides when you should get up—usually a lot earlier than you might have chosen. If you're lucky, your cat awakens you gently with a hesitant paw to the cheek; if you're unlucky, your cat regards you as a six-foot mouse that needs to be pounced on with all fours.

I despised cat people. My sister was one. Her first felines were Peanut Butter and Jelly. They were eventually supplanted by Fred and Ginger. One Christmas, as a stocking stuffer, I gave her a bumper sticker I'd gotten at a truck stop: *Cats Flattened While You Wait.*

But everything changed in the fall of 1984. Until then, I'd written a dozen books in an office that measured nine by fifteen feet. My writing companions were our golden retriever, Tiffany, and her daughter, Strawberry, who was half Irish wolfhound (someone had forgotten to latch the kennel gate). We lived at Rock Harbor, right on the water at the inner crook of Cape Cod Bay.

By the summer of '84, thanks largely to royalties from *The Light and the Glory*, which I'd coauthored with Peter Marshall, we were able to do some serious house renovation. My writer friend Jamie Buckingham once told me that if I ever had the money, I ought to do the Irish thing and get up high: "Build a tower and leave only enough room on the top floor for yourself and your desk."

I took his advice. After we got done doubling my wife's closet space, we built a lighthouse on the end of the house. It looked like the real thing. And to get to the top floor, where I had a swiveling admiral's chair surrounded by desk and 360 degrees of view, you had to go up a ship's ladder. It was open like a regular ladder, but with steps instead of rungs.

The dogs refused to go up it. "This is ridiculous!" I chided Tiffany. "All over the Cape are construction guys with red pickup trucks and golden retrievers. Their dogs go up *real* ladders, with rungs."

If Tiff would go, her daughter would follow. But she would not be shamed.

"Okay, we'll do this the old-fashioned way, with bribery." I put a MilkBone on each step. Tiff would whimper and eat them until she got to the top. But then she would not come down, even for Milk-Bones. She whined and wailed until I finally carried her down. And Strawberry, spooked by it all, would not even get near the ladder.

I had two choices, neither of them appealing. I could either write alone, or heed Samuel Johnson's advice: "If you would write, keep cats." (Google credits Aldous Huxley, but Dr. Johnson said it first.)

I was going to have to change my mind about cats. The very thought made me shudder. How could an ailurophobe (cat-hater) be transformed into an ailurophile overnight? It would take a miracle.

Fortunately, being a praying person, I knew someone in the miracle business. I put it to Him: "Since this seems to be your solution, you pick the cat."

The next day a schoolteacher friend mentioned a litter that was up for adoption. That was quick, I had to admit. But I still wasn't sold on the idea. I called and made an appointment to go see them. The litter was in Wellfleet, two towns away. I went there first thing the next morning.

The lawn needed mowing, and as I went up to the front door, I noticed a half-empty two-liter bottle of Coke on the front step. Judging from the elaborate spider's web affixed to it and the step, it had been there awhile. Quite a while. I rang the bell. The door was opened by a large woman in a food-stained muumuu, a cigarette hanging from her lip.

"I'm here about the cat."

She nodded and waved me in. "They are eight of them." As she spoke, I could see one of them darting behind a sofa. My nose, normally deaf, had already informed me that the whole house was apparently their litter box.

"I'd like a female." Our dogs and my family's dogs had all been females. They seemed a little less willful, a little more tractable.

"There'd be four of those. Take your pick."

"Um, I'm new at this, differentiating between male and female kittens. Could you possibly . . ."

She shrugged. "I'll put the females in there," she said, indicating a packing crate in the kitchen. Then she started rounding them up. I stood beside the refrigerator, watching her. And panicking. What was I thinking of? I hated cats! This was going against all my instincts.

On top of the fridge, at my eye level, was a two-thirds-eaten Sara Lee chocolate cake. Into the remaining third someone had stubbed out a cigarette. (I am not making this up.) *That's it,* I thought. *I'm outta here!* "Uh, ma'am? I think maybe I'd better—"

She seemed not to hear me. Smiling (and blocking my exit), she pointed to the box. "Got 'em all now. Cute, aren't they?"

Well, they *were* cute. Tiny, tumbling balls of fur, full of curiosity and play. Big, opalescent eyes that made them look like wee owls. My heart softened.

"They seem—small," I observed. "How old are they?"

"Six weeks."

"Isn't that a little young to be leaving their mother?"

"They can see—they can go." (I learned later that to complete the bonding process, kittens should not leave their mother until the tenth week.)

Reaching down into the box, I tried to touch one of them. Immediately a scrawny nervous one, littler than the rest, came over and made a great fuss over my extended hand. I scooped her up and looked at her face. She almost seemed to be begging me to take her with me. I knew I was being anthropomorphic, but she was being awfully persuasive.

Then I remembered my pact with God. He was to pick the cat. *Is it this one?* I asked inwardly, holding the nervous one up for His inspection.

In my heart I seemed to hear, *It is the quiet one in the corner.* I looked at that one—tiger-striped, solemnly watching all the goings-on. Unmoved and not moving.

Putting the nervous one down, I picked up the quiet one and gazed into her bright blue, gemstone eyes. They were amazingly iridescent.

Before I could say anything, the woman reassured me. "They won't be that color much longer. They'll be mostly green, like their mother's."

I sighed; I was going to do this. "Well, I'll take this one."

"I thought you liked the little one."

I nodded. "I did. But this is the one I want."

The woman suddenly smiled. "Why don't you take them both? They can keep each other company."

I thought about that. Not long. "We're a dog family. This is our first cat. We'll start with one."

We found something to take her home in: an empty Kleenex box with Scotch tape over the opening.

When I got home there was no one else in the house. In the kitchen, with the door to the garage firmly shut, I took her out of the Kleenex box. On impulse I put her on the food scale: sixteen ounces. Whoa, *really* small. And—I sniffed her—*really* dirty.

A bath would fix that. I took her to the upstairs bathroom and carefully closed the door behind me. What to use—something mild, like Johnson's baby shampoo. But it had been a long time since there'd been any babies in the house; the best I could come up with was my teenage daughter's Breck shampoo, "For dry and damaged hair."

The basin was not large, but we were dealing with a very small cat. I filled the sink with lukewarm water, checking its temperature on the inside of my wrist, like I used to with formula bottles a long time ago.

We were ready. At least, I was. Cat, sitting on the counter observing the preparations, was dubious in the extreme. Water was good for drinking, but a little went a long way. What we were looking at in the sink was a lifetime's supply.

The moment of truth had come. Holding her firmly with both hands, I briefly dunked her in.

She was appalled! Eyes bulging out of her head, she stuck her limbs straight out and hissed mightily.

I was shaken by this response. But not stirred. I explained to her calmly but a little tensely, "Cat, we're going to do this. It's the only way to get you clean, and I'm a whole lot bigger than you are."

She tried to wriggle away. Holding her on her back with my right hand, I grabbed the shampoo bottle and squeezed a dollop on her stomach and worked it in. More hissing. More wriggling. But before long I had her sudsed all over. I dunked her again to get the soap off and noticed that there was a gray residue around the rim of the basin. I sighed. We were going to have to do this again.

Setting her on the floor, I cleaned out the basin, which was really foul, and got a fresh bath ready.

But when I went to get her, I couldn't find her. Impossible! Then I saw the tip of a tiny tail protruding from behind the toilet. Grabbing it, I dragged her out. And we went through the whole process again. This time when we got done the bathwater was clear. And she passed the close-up sniff test.

I dried her off with the guest towel we were never supposed to use. I got her dry, but I couldn't stop her shaking with cold, and all the rubbing in the world could not warm her up. This was serious. *Now what?*

What came to me was to use a blow-dryer. In the bottom drawer of the sink cabinet, I found my daughter's. It worked. Cat was terrified. This thing hissed louder than she ever had.

But it did the job. She stopped shaking and was soon at room temperature. I looked at her and had to laugh; her fur was all spikey. But it was dry, and she was warm. Enough.

All at once, as if to concur, she yawned. I made a nest for her with the other guest towel and put her in it. She stayed.

Ducking out, I closed the door gently but firmly behind me and shooed downstairs the curious canines who'd been standing outside the bathroom. From the trunk of my car I retrieved the cat stuff I'd obtained before going to fetch Cat. It was going in the lighthouse, but I hadn't set it up because I didn't know if I'd have any need of it.

On the first floor of the lighthouse I set up the litter box, along with dry food and water. What to do for a bed? I emptied a book carton and trimmed down its sides with a utility knife. For a lining, I parted with an old friend, a hole-y cashmere sweater that three times my wife had tried to throw away.

I was ready. I went and got the newest member of our family and brought her over to the lighthouse and installed her. She seemed to appreciate the bed, and still exhausted from the morning's adventures, she curled up and went to sleep.

I went up the ship's ladder and, turning on a Mozart string quartet, did my best to make America's westward expansion interesting and fun to read. But my mind kept going back to the little creature on the floor below. All I wanted to do was go down and look at her.

*Get your chapter done,* I upbraided myself. My co-writer, Peter, was coming over in three hours. I gazed out the north window. It was a clear day; I could make out the Provincetown tower nineteen miles away. What should we name her? Naming a pet was serous business. You could go cute, like my sister. Or wry. Or something else. (Years later, when I had a brother and sister from the same litter, I went to the Twenty-Third Psalm and named them Goodness and Mercy. Later, when they were joined by a male, I named him Surely. He was not happy about that; it sounded like a girl's name. I assured him that in England there were many men named Shirley. Manly men. He wouldn't come to it, even when I took care to pronounce it in a manly way. So I nicknamed him Bumper, because he was generous with his head bumps.)

But what to call this one? The lighthouse was going to be her home, mostly. What do you call a Lighthouse cat?

I said it aloud, "The lighthouse cat, _____." Nothing. I said it again, adding a little Edgar Allan Poe reverb. There was only one name to end that refrain: Esmeralda.

"Esmeralda!" I exclaimed. "Ezzie, or Ez, for short."

I heard a little scritching behind me. And there she was, two steps from the top of the ladder. She would stretch up with her forepaws to the next step, and with all her might, do a sort of cat chin-up. When she reached the top step, she was tired enough to let me pick her up and hold her in my lap, stroking her till she purred.

---

### Do Cats Really Hate Water?

No. That's a myth. What cats actually hate is *cold* water. Many a cat swims in the family pool in the sun or enjoys the warm spray of his human's morning shower. It is true that most cats don't like to be bathed, but that's more about losing control over their physical circumstances—and possibly a human who isn't thinking like a cat when bathing him.

---

# Small and Mighty, Great and Good

*Jeanette Thomason*

Our little farm in Washington State had plenty of strays from neighbors up the road, and more left behind by migrant workers in our valley of apple orchards. The strays would spend a day in our barn and a night at the neighbor's. They would play under the apple trees and in the wooden crates stacked for harvest. But they didn't really belong to anyone—appearing, multiplying, and disappearing like rabbits from the hats of a magic act. Our other animals at the farm were more permanent. We had cattle grazing the alfalfa pastures, a little Scottie-mix terrier who guarded our house and garden, two guinea pigs who lived in the laundry room and served as living garbage disposals of the day's carrot peelings and lettuce cores, and the occasional pigs in a pen behind the barn. We just never had a cat of our very own, and in particular never a house cat.

Our mother was about to change that. She was all about taking strays in, whether four-legged or two, from the wayfarer to, once, a boy who ran away from home and hid between the outbuildings along our pasture. She was the kind of woman who always had an extra pillow for one who needed a place to lay his head, and she grew up in a home where it was customary to set an extra place at the table for anyone who might drop in at dinner. So Mom was ready when a co-worker told how she was allergic to fur and didn't know how to help her daughter who was moving to England and could not take along her long-haired cat.

Mom broached our father with the story. "Can we take it? It could help with the snakes in the pasture."

"Okay," Dad answered. "But the cat doesn't come in the house."

Our father didn't believe in animals living under the same roof as their people. "They have a place of their own," he said—a whole world, God's green earth. "They get along better than you think in the outdoors. They're made for it." In the wild, he added, God's good creatures could be about His business, just as we are to be about our own. That meant if a whale should swallow a prophet now and then from the ocean depths in order to get the Word to the people, so be it. Likewise, should the brook trout bite our fishing lines, the fish would feed us through summer. Should the cow, lying in the shade, chew her cud, this was to produce milk for our cereal. Should the pig, in its pen, eat his corn and play in the mud, it was to build the muscle to make the bacon lean. Dad emphasized: Let all creatures, even the little ones, do what they were made to do.

The message was not lost on us. The cat, if we were to have one, should live in the barn and scare away the snakes and kill the vermin. This was the cat's job, the cat's purpose, the cat's destiny.

So after work the next day, Mom went to collect the cat with Betty, who carpooled with her into town. Betty would be in charge of holding the cat on their way home.

The exchange itself was uneventful, as Mom tells it: A simple introduction. City Kitty, meet Farm Wife. Then some scant instruction like "the cat has never been outdoors" and "likes to be brushed" and "is very friendly." I imagine Mom, who was on her feet and on the go most of the time, liked these ideas, the glamour of them, especially the one of resting with a beautiful cat on her lap, brushing its long coat into a glossy shine. Of course, doing this would mean the cat would sometimes be indoors. Before Mom could think how to manage that, the girl giving up the cat interrupted.

She cried and hugged the cat farewell. She carried on a bit, surprising for someone so willing to give up her pet.

"Good-bye, Rhubarb," she finally sobbed.

"Rhubarb?" Mom checked. "Like the pie?"

"No," the girl said. Her sobbing stopped, she matter-of-factly stated, "Rhubarb. You know. Like in baseball."

Mom didn't know, but planned to ask Dad when she got home. This might earn the cat extra favor since our dad was a great baseball enthusiast. He loved the game since youth, and associated all things in baseball with pleasure and leisure. This was good, Mom thought. She hugged the cat close, and Rhubarb, completely trusting, leaned into her. Mom stroked the little cat's chest and headed to the car she'd left idling.

Rhubarb, indeed friendly, leaned in a little more with each firm stroke down her back. But when the car door opened, she decided something was seriously wrong. Her body went rigid.

This was not a house but some smaller enclosure that purred in a strange way. She protested a little with an outreached leg as she was passed from my mother's arms into Betty's.

Mom commented on how good Rhubarb was: "Not even a yowl."

Rhubarb didn't have to. A silent protest can be even more deadly. Mom drove the entire forty-five minutes home with Betty soaked and stinking of cat urine.

"Good luck," Betty said, handing Rhubarb back to Mom at the farm. Mom headed for the back door, carrying in outstretched arms a stinking Rhubarb, as Betty (Stinking Betty, she then called herself) trotted across the road to her home.

"Kitchen," Mom pronounced to us as we paraded after her, the cat, held at arm's length, leading the way like a long-haired mermaid at the helm of a great ship on a new adventure. "Now, get me the shampoo but stand clear."

My brother and I watched the show as Mom used the sprayer at the kitchen sink to wash Stinking Rhubarb. The cat was no longer good, nor quiet, nor glamorous. She was just wet and unhappy. Drenched and ruined, she growled, first in low tones but quickly escalated to high-pitched yowls. She spat and fought the shampoo, her glamour washing down the drain with the stink. Our mom, just five-foot-three, struggled to hold Rhubarb, who seemed surprisingly slight, at half her dry size, for all the fight in her.

Mom voiced as much. "How can a thing so small be so mighty?" She massaged Rhubarb's face. Rhubarb would have none of the soothing till she was out of the sink and away from the water. She made a right hook with her claws, slicing Mom's arm, leaving four long tracks that drew blood. Mom made one last pass with the water sprayer, then swooped and swaddled the cat into a towel, tucking those fierce claws tight into the folds.

Rhubarb looked dazed and every bit the barn cat now. Her glorious long, fluffy coat hung like a wet wall of matted white-and-gray-spotted hair. Her muscles tensed and twitched. You could feel the energy beneath the sodden legs, ready to spring the instant that towel was loosened. She stared us down with eyes of green, eyes translucent as marbles that saw beyond the surface, to the bone of things.

No question. The understanding between the four of us was crystal: This was a baptism. All things were new.

I was first to speak. Should we begin with the name? *Rhubarb* seemed a ridiculous one. "Why would anyone ever name such a beautiful cat *Rhubarb*?" The name baffled me. "It doesn't fit."

"Maybe it does," Dad said later, head cocked, one eyebrow slightly raised as he looked at the cat in Mom's scratched arms. He explained that in baseball, the term *rhubarb* means a squabble, a fuss, an outright brawl.

We stared silently at Rhubarb, now calm and incredibly fluffy again in Mom's lap: the black-rimmed eyes, the boa-like tail, the heart-shaped face.

Dad voiced what we were thinking: "But she doesn't look like a fighter."

She didn't that evening, either, when we marched her out to the barn, a parade that once again she led, this time swaddled and held close to Mom's chest, no longer the mermaid at the helm of a ship, just an anxious little cat pointed toward some deep unknown.

In a front corner of the barn, Dad made a little bed from an old apple box. We filled it with hay and Mom covered it with an old pillow and blankets. We tucked in Rhubarb and whispered good-night in her ear. Then Dad shuttered the barn windows and secured the doors so she couldn't wander into the night.

"It doesn't seem right, making her sleep out here," I pouted as we paraded back to the house. I had been lobbying for Rhubarb to remain an indoor cat. I shared my mom's ideas for the glamour, only many more degrees of it. Besides, I pleaded my case, there were spiders in the barn, and mice. It was dirty and musty. It was dark, except for the blue wash of a gleaming moon filtering through the eaves.

"The barn won't bother her a bit," Dad said. "The spiders and mice will give her something to chase. Just wait. You'll see."

The next morning my brother and I raced to the barn. We found Rhubarb curled into a nest she'd fixed just so. She looked up at us, very still, eyes fixed with caution, every muscle tensed.

My brother scooped her up to his chest and tucked her into his overalls to head back to the house. As we approached the gate between the pasture and backyard, we could see a family of California quail scattered underneath the large weeping birch tree. Their black top hats, little question-mark-shaped plumes, bobbed up and down as they pecked at the seed scattered there. Rhubarb's gaze fixed on the tide of plumes washing across the lawn. Instinctively, her eyes widened. Her pupils grew from inky slits to pools that reflected the titters and bobs of a dozen balls of feathers.

At the creak of the gate, one of the quail brethren, the watchman sitting atop a fence post, jerked his head. He scrammed down the fence post. Rhubarb twitched. She struggled to pop out of Greg's overalls as a kaleidoscope of quail spread from beneath the tree. Arms and legs flailing, she scratched at Greg's neck for traction, then leaped from his arms, now raised in surrender. She landed on all fours and froze. The quail, so speedy on spinning legs, had scattered and disappeared. Rhubarb's head spun around in an effort to zero-in on at least one panicked bird.

She should have been disappointed. Instead, she stayed fixed on the grass, hips slightly raised, tail sweeping the lawn, nose twitching. She remained frozen and tingling there at the same time. Slowly, a smile, big as the Cheshire's, spread across her heart-shaped face. The scurry had awakened—for lack of a better term—all her catness.

I felt awakened myself. Through her eyes and her newfound senses, the earth sprung alive. The grass smelled sweeter, the air fresher. Everyday sounds amplified: the chug of irrigation sprinklers, the trills of songbirds, the chirp of crickets. The whole backyard seemed to hum a concert of summer.

My brother and I stretched out on the grass. Greg and I watched drifting clouds change shape, and Rhubarb stared down the feeder for wayward birds. She swatted at a miller moth and buried her nose deep into the grass to take in every last scent of an earthy world she was claiming as hers.

Lazy day slipped into evening as she investigated all corners of the backyard. We moved the apple-crate bed that night to the back porch. We didn't worry she would wander back to the city. She sat on the back porch, flicking her tail under glittery stars. She had discovered a whole new world of her own, God's green earth. She would get along better than we thought.

As summer turned to fall, Rhubarb learned to walk on fences, play hide-and-seek with the strays, and luxuriate in sun baths on the back porch. On insufferably hot days she claimed a cool spot of earth under the lilacs, where she wore the earth into a perfect cat-sized bowl. She'd flatten herself there, in wait of the returning train of quail with their pea-sized brains. Her other favorite place to lurk for birds and creeping things was in the alfalfa field on the other side of the backyard fence.

It was there that she was in wait of field mice on one of those last hot days of September.

Mom and I were fixing dinner and Dad was trying out the new sickle mower for the tractor on a last hay cut of the season. The new sickle rolled silently through the pasture, reaching farther than the rattling, noisy old one.

Mom saw everything from the kitchen window: the silent sickle, the methodical tractor, Rhubarb limping from the pasture and across the back lawn, a line of blood streaming behind her. Mom screamed and ran out the back door, calling Dad's name. I followed, waving my arms to catch his attention. He shut off the motor and raced to the back porch, where we huddled on the steps.

Whether in shock or resignation, Rhubarb never fought as Mom and Dad cleaned the wound, applied pressure and an analgesic antibiotic cream, then wrapped her back leg, now a stub, in a mummy-like dressing. Mom rocked her, swaddled and cradled like a baby. Rhubarb's three feet pointed to heaven, like a prayer.

"Poor thing," we took turns whispering.

It turned out the cut had been right through the bone, so clean at the ankle that the leg was not damaged. Within a week the wound healed over; within two weeks the scab shrunk. In another three weeks, fur began to grow around the nub.

We'd kept Rhubarb in the apple box on the back step, where we could check on her every few hours and doctor the leg, applying the healing creams, massaging her back and limbs. She rested at first, but it wasn't long before she wanted to be hobbling around. We assembled a conglomeration of apple crates to form a pen, to keep her safe, protect her from more harm.

She did not understand "poor thing." She hopped across the barricades as soon as we put them up, and then stalked from patio to lawn. She tired of the bandages and began to gnaw them. She was ready to reclaim the world, her farm world, for all its danger.

Who could blame her? September in the foothills of the Cascades brings all kinds of beauty: the orchards in harvest, the fruit ripe and heavy, squash and pumpkins coloring the last of everyone's gardens, leaves changing on trees and twirling down into a crunchy carpet. Even as the calendar tells the world it should be going dormant, God's green earth determines to come alive in a new way, hum a new song.

So did our cat. Though missing a piece of herself, she seemed to find more of who she was and remind us more of what we all should be about. This was never more clear than one September long after the one when she lost that back left foot. Rhubarb had grown old, and I watched her sit on the back step before sunrise. She always waited there for Dad, who rose in the dark and pulled on tall rubber irrigation boots with one hand, and with the other scooped her close for the long walk to the barn. She no longer hunted for mice, but she never gave up watching for the slow-witted quail. She never gave up on watching Dad go about the morning chores, either: giving grain to the cattle, checking the water tanks, and, in summer, cutting the wild asparagus that grew along the irrigation ditches. She waited for him to pick her up again, small enough to be carried in one hand, so small that as she leaned in to the bib of Dad's overalls, only legs askew showed. Small yet mighty is the heart that would rest even in the hands of the one who, unwittingly, was the driver behind her disaster.

Cats, we're told, have nine lives. Rhubarb, I believe, came to show us what to do with our one, for danger is always close at hand, or underfoot, as the case may be. And so is grace.

*three red-winged blackbirds*
*dive-bomb the neighbor's tomcat*
*who wisely moves on*

# Buster's Heaven on Earth

*Cathy E. Watkins*

Hey, I'm Buster, a middle-aged yellow Persian cat with no front claws and an attitude of Who Gives a Rip. I live with the Watkins family in a house with many windows. Talk about heaven. I'm running a household on a lake with more bird feeders than I've ever seen and all the food I can eat. My day is full of planning how I'm going to capture the many birds, chipmunks, squirrels, and flies around here, and then what I'm going to do with them. Well, if I could get at them, that is. . . .

I share my heaven with humans and beasts. I tolerate Lexi, the Shih Tzu, and Angel, the outdoor cat. No sense wishing I could go outside. Ain't gonna happen. My job is more important than being able to live outside, anyway.

These days my life consists of running the household, eating, and napping. I am very good at napping, by the way. So how did I get such a good life? Trust me, it didn't come easy. That is, what I remember.

I don't know what my name was back then because my memories of my first years of life are vague. I only recall pain and lots of competition for food, attention, and shelter. My diet consisted of whatever was left over after everyone else was finished. I don't remember how I lost my front claws. After contracting a kidney infection that caused me to start doing my thing outside the box, my humans put me outdoors to fend for myself. That did not go well, and the next thing I knew I woke up at a vet hospital with a shaved body and stitches down my side and hip. I was a sorrowful sight and very lucky that a great organization rescued me, saw fit to get me medical attention, and looked for a new home for me.

Do you know how hard and embarrassing it is as a Persian cat to establish my role as the boss when I'm shaved, clawless, and homeless? I lost my voice from the shame, and no matter how hard I try, I cannot meow or warn you to keep your distance. Nevertheless, I have mastered The Look. That will stop you in your tracks. And my purr box works overtime and is really loud. I would rather have a good purr than a good meow any day.

Everyone in my new place continually mentioned my unique personality and loving ways. My caretakers named me Jazz. Waiting for a forever home meant living in an office inside a crate while I healed and tried to let the dogs around me know who was the boss. I was not in my best shape, so that is where I perfected The Look.

My luck continued to improve when a lady named Cathy adopted me. She felt a cat would be low maintenance and good company for her eighty-year-old mother. Don't want to throw a wrench into anyone's plan, but I'm not sure the tripping factor was considered beforehand. Even I know eighty-year-old humans don't move very fast, and their balance is a bit unstable. But who listens to a cat—especially a cat who cannot talk.

My new owner renamed me Taz because she didn't quite catch on to the Jazz thing. Living in my new home was much better than being kept in a crate in an office, and there were many places to explore. The windows were a bit hard to see out of, but I was happy to be safe with nobody to fight for my food. I healed up, my hair grew out, and I bonded with my new owner, giving and getting much love in the meantime. Still no voice, but my purr box made up for it. After a couple weeks I was given a new name. I was now called Buster. That was the nickname of her son who died a few years back. I like the name Buster, and I answer to it now. It goes very well with The Look.

I thought this would be my home for a long time, and I was very happy and at peace with where events had taken me. But I do have my shortcomings, and I guess the biggest one is that when it comes to food, I run short on patience. Not being able to meow and tell you what I need means I have to touch you and get in your way to get the message across. While doing this one morning, with my belly growling for breakfast, I somehow caused a trip hazard. My new eighty-year-old friend got in my way and hit the floor. They hauled her off to the hospital. I felt bad. I am still not sure how they thought this was my fault, but I figured it would be back to the office and the crate for me. I did hope that, until then, people would open all the window blinds for me.

Over the next few weeks and then a month I had the house to myself. Cathy would come feed me, water me, and clean my pan. Not a lot going on. Even though I was content, I was not happy. I need excitement, entertainment, and someone to rub me when I want it. So it was quiet and lonely until the day Cathy came and put me back in my crate, gathered up all my stuff, and took me to the car.

I didn't know where I was going or how I would manage.

The ride took a while, and I was sure I was going back to that office for another try at another family. But when the car stopped and we got out, there it was: heaven on earth. I could see that my new home had lots of windows, more bird feeders than I had ever seen, and—wait a minute . . . other animals? A dog? Another cat? I just hoped they didn't think they were the boss and I was their slave. Never! Not me. Then I wondered what their names were. . . .

Settling in was easy for me but challenging for the others. Lexi, the Shih Tzu, is a spoiled brat, and Angel, with the claws, thinks she is all that and a pot of catnip. But I knew they'd find out soon enough that I'm a bit of a bully and would rule the roost.

It's going okay now. I'm pretty sure I am now in my forever home. I don't have to worry about being hurt or not being fed. My hair is back to full length, my injuries all healed, I eat only the good stuff, and I get attention whenever I want it.

I try not to gloat, but I hear the humans say that I have brought much happiness to their lives and am very entertaining. Everyone who meets me has kind things to say. And even though I don't have claws, I have a mean right jab. Just bring on any attitude and I will wallop you with both front paws. I have earned my place and given much love back in return. I know that if anything happens, there are other people standing in line to take me in.

Now if I could just get outside that window, I would show that squirrel who's boss. . . .

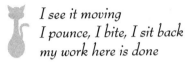

*I see it moving*
*I pounce, I bite, I sit back*
*my work here is done*

# How an Abandoned Cat Changed My Life

## Dusty Rainbolt

When I answered the phone that night in 1986, a six-inch blanket of snow covered the ground in north Texas. That almost never happens—the snow, I mean. I do answer my phone about twenty times a day.

"You busy?" my friend Mary asked. She sounded anxious. I'd met Mary several years earlier at a science-fiction convention. I thought she'd called to read me excerpts from her latest short story. It turned out to be a real-life adventure, and I would claim the leading role.

Mary had found a hungry cat trembling next to the front door of her apartment. Obviously someone had moved away and left the little silver tabby cat behind *in the snow* to fend for herself. Mary, who was not an animal person but has a heart as big as Texas, brought the starving kitty into her apartment to thaw her out. With a $500 pet deposit threatening her, the

Hamilton home could only offer emergency shelter. The sooner the abandoned kitty could go elsewhere, the better.

"Can you take her? She's a really nice cat," Mary assured me. *She must be an amazing cat for Mary to take such a risk*, I thought. I uttered an uncertain, "Okay . . ."

Before the second syllable had completely escaped my mouth, Mary added, "Did I forget to mention the cat's a little pregnant?"

"How can she be 'a little pregnant'?"

Mary ignored the question and thanked me for taking care of her big problem.

"What, pray, qualifies me to take a pregnant cat?" I asked.

"You already have a cat," Mary said.

After two weeks it became clear little Mom kitty's big moment was drawing nigh. Mom began scoping out the house for the perfect nest. I felt like Prissy in *Gone with the Wind* who didn't know nothin' 'bout birthing no babies! Being an inexperienced midwife, I decided to preempt the cat's quest by creating a soft nursery of a cardboard box; clean, well-aged (translate that to mean bleached-out) towels; and an old cerise bedspread, the kind that wouldn't show stains. Mom immediately hopped out of her lowly box and headed straight for my lingerie drawer. Birthing felines always prefer lingerie simply because silk is by far more difficult to clean than terry cloth.

Mom brought six beautiful, healthy kittens into the world. She'd strewn her first three around the house like clues on a treasure map. She deposited one slimy little ball of fur on my desk, making a direct hit on a recently completed 1040 form. I found another one under the commode, and, of course, one comfortably wrapped in my beige silk camisole. Mom managed to completely avoid dropping any of her bundles in the bedding I had laid out for them. We compromised with her three remaining kittens, and she gave birth to them on the soft blanket spread out in the bathtub.

Mom must have been shameless. No two kittens looked alike, nor did they even remotely resemble her. There was one the color of fresh cream, one was all black, and a third resembled a patchwork blanket. The one born on the tax form looked like Florida citrus, while another looked like pewter. And the smallest, and my favorite, was black and white.

Within just a few minutes of her final delivery, Mom had once again transferred the whole group back to her silk and lace haven. I gave up. You can't fight Kitty Hall. Besides, it gave me the perfect excuse to go out and buy a new set of undies.

Those kittens weren't afraid of anything. When they grew big enough, they prowled the house like a pack of wild hyenas. On several occasions the Wild Bunch cornered my eighty-pound Doberman in the utility room and used his hind leg as a climbing tree. They emptied my goldfish bowl, and one even took a swim in my toilet. Whenever I left the house I had to incarcerate the little offenders—or else I'd just have to up the value on my homeowner's insurance. When I returned from work I swung open the bathroom door and allowed the prisoners to escape. Every time, the black-and-white one, who I named Chani after the protagonist in my first novel, would prance out the door, look over her shoulder, and let out a loud, indignant meow.

It soon came time to find homes for Mom and her brood. Like everything else in life, this proved to be much more complicated than I had originally anticipated. Friends and family claimed to have all the pets they needed, so I had to think outside the litter box. I enlisted the help of the Humane Society of Lewisville, the only no-kill rescue group north of Dallas. McDonald's in Lewisville was the only place that would give us permission to hold adoption events in their parking lot, so I religiously took the kitties to Adopt-A-Pets, all of us baking under the hot Texas sun.

As I sat in that steamy parking lot with a handful of other cat fosters, I realized that there were so many cats who needed families. The small rescue group simply didn't have enough foster homes. I was haunted by the kitties the group picked up from animal control but had to return to the shelter, to a short and certain future when they didn't get adopted. Although it was a small one, the one-afternoon adoption event at least gave those hopeless kitties a chance they wouldn't have had at the pound.

After my second Adopt-A-Pet, Mom and four of the kittens found loving homes. My two favorites, Chani and Reggie, failed to get adopted, mainly because I kept "forgetting" to take them to McDonald's. (My two kittens would make it to seventeen and nineteen years respectively.)

Once the kittens went to forever homes, I offered to foster a doomed silver-colored pound kitten I named Seryi—Russian for *blue*. The little cutie got adopted very quickly. Since Seryi's adoption made room in my house, I took in another, then another. I couldn't help just one!

Mom and her babies waltzed into my life twenty-five years ago. I guess that means I'm now eligible for my silver water bowl. I've suffered from foster failure several times along the way, but most of the kitties were adopted into great homes.

I even married a guy who had more kitties than I had and who feels as passionate about saving homeless cats as I do. On our third date we rescued a three-week-old abandoned kitten.

My full-time job is now editing and writing about cat (pet) care for AdoptAShelter.com, a shop-to-donate website that helps animal charities. And I still rescue. I now take in primarily bottle babies and trauma cases. Today, five eight-week-old kittens are cliff-diving off the back of my antique recliner and torturing the dog. A Siamese coyote-attack survivor is snoozing comfortably in my guest bathroom.

I think back twenty-five years as I look at photos of Chani and Reggie. These pictures serve as a constant reminder that a prudent person does not take in pregnant felines, but a soft touch always does. I can't believe how saving that one little abandoned mama has changed my life. Where would I be, what would I be doing had I told my friend to take the cat to the pound? I shudder to think.

Mary still calls, but she has never asked me to take another orphan. However, at least once a week I get calls from animal control asking for help. And sometimes, when I open my door, I find a frightened mother-to-be with sad eyes and no collar around her neck. I just bring out the cerise blanket and my silk camisole. Some people never learn.

# Acknowledgments

What can I say about an editor who at any given time has several cats and a few dogs living in her home? And who at the same time manages to acquire and edit bestselling books? I can simply say that she *is* the best, and I am a lucky person to have her for my editor. Thank you, Vicki Crumpton, for all your support and guidance.

Many thanks to the gifted staff in the editorial, marketing, publicity, sales, and art departments at Revell, a division of Baker Publishing Group, for their vision and hard work. It's a privilege to be part of this team.

And many thanks to Dwight Baker, president of Baker Publishing Group and a man who clearly loves and respects the beasts of the earth.

# Notes

1. Sue Manning, "Paw Preference Tests Can Be Fun for Pets," *Jackson Citizen Patriot*, 9/11/12, D5.

2. Rob Elliott, *Zoolarious Animal Jokes for Kids* (Grand Rapids, MI: Revell, 2012).

3. John V. Dennis, "The House Cat Sheds Its Image," *The Conservationist*, May/June 1980, 39.

4. Christina Boufis, "Kitty Checkups," *WebMDPets Magazine*, Fall 2011, 69.

# About the Contributors

**Donna Acton** is a licensed veterinary technician who has worked in veterinary hospitals for over three decades. As the daughter of a veterinarian, she has had a lifelong interest in helping pets and the people they live with, and her professional focus now is behavior training for dogs and cats.

**Pam Allnutt** is a visual artist and teacher from Wheaton, Illinois. She lives with her husband, Rick, and Winston T. Cat, a muted tiger whose delight in small things reminds them daily of the joys to be found in everyday life.

**Robert Benson** has written more than a dozen books about the search for the Holy in the midst of our everyday lives, work critically acclaimed in publications as diverse as the *New York Times*, *Publishers Weekly*, and *American Benedictine Review*. He lives, writes, pays attention to, and is monitored closely by the Monk in Nashville, Tennessee. More information is available at www.robertbensonwriter.com.

**Melody Carlson** (www.melodycarlson.com) is one of the most prolific novelists of our day. With around 200 books published and sales topping 5.5 million, Melody writes primarily for women and teens. She's won numerous honors and awards, including The Rita, Gold Medallion, Carol Award, and Romantic Times Lifetime Achievement award, and some of her books are being considered for TV movies. Melody has two grown sons and makes her home in the Pacific Northwest with her husband, Chris, their Maine coon, Harry, and yellow Lab, Audrey.

**Sandy Cathcart** is a lover of all things wild. She lives in the highlands of Southern Oregon with her husband, Charlie (the Cat Man), where she paints and writes about her adventures. Her book *Wild Woman: A Daughter's Search for a Father's Love* is available at Amazon or on her website at www.sandycathcart.com.

**Cindy Crosby's** idea of a good time is to curl up on the couch with a stack of library books, her husband, Jeff, and their cat, Socks. She's the author or compiler of seven books, including *By Willoway Brook,* and a contributor to eight others. Her writing has appeared in *Backpacker, Books & Culture,* and *Publishers Weekly,* and her books have been featured in *Chicago Wilderness, Orion,* the *Chicago Sun-Times,* and *NBC Chicago.* Find out more at www.cindycrosby.com.

**Vicki Crumpton** has over twenty years of publishing experience. She holds an MDiv and a PhD and works from her home in Western Kentucky. When she's not taking care of the menagerie, you can often find her riding a bike, paddling a kayak, or taking photos.

**Andrea Doering** is an editor, wife, mother of three, and happy resident of a town full of cats.

**Lonnie Hull DuPont** is a poet, a writer of nonfiction, and a book editor. Her poetry, which can be read in dozens of periodicals and literary journals, has won many awards and has been nominated for a Pushcart Prize. She is also the author of *The Haiku Box*. She and her husband, Joe, are owned by two brilliant and beautiful felines who make them slow down and pay attention.

**Callie Smith Grant** loves animals of all kinds. She is the author of many animal stories, the author of several books for young readers, and the compiler of the anthologies *The Dog Next Door*, *A Prince among Dogs*, and *A Dickens of a Cat*.

**Marilyn Guidinger** grew up on a farm in southeastern Pennsylvania with many cats that she individually named and cared for. After obtaining a degree in chemistry, she worked in the environmental testing field and traveled widely in the States and in Europe. Now retired, she volunteers as the office manager of a historic theater in Jackson, Michigan, and serves as the chair of the Jackson Historic District Commission. While she does not currently have a cat companion, she does volunteer at the local Humane Society.

**Alison Hodgson's** writing has been featured on houzz.com; Her.meneutics, the *Christianity Today* blog for women; Religion News Service; and praiseandcoffee.com. She reviews books for the Dove Foundation and has been blogging since 2005 at olderthanjesus.blogspot.com. She lives with her husband, their three children, and two good dogs in Michigan.

**Donna Hollingsworth** is a high school history teacher. For many years she taught ballet in her own school of dance after trouping with a ballet company in New York City. Donna is a lover of all animals and usually has at least four or more pets at a time. She lives in the Pocono Mountains with her family.

**Pamela Lione** is a novelist and screenwriter and a native New Yorker. She is the author of four novels in the Midtown Blue Series: *The Deuce, The Crossroads, Skells,* and *Clear Blue Sky.* Pam has written for both television and film and currently has a motion picture in development. She and her husband, Frank, have residences in Manhattan's Hell's Kitchen neighborhood and in Pennsylvania. They have two dear sons, Georgie and Frankie, and a golden retriever named Buddy.

**Kathi Lipp** is the author of eight books including *Praying God's Word for Your Life* and *The Husband Project.* She speaks all over the country but always comes home to her husband, Roger; their cats, Zorro and Ashley; and their puggle, Jake. For loads of free recipes, tips, and way too many cat pictures, check out www.kathilipp.com.

The late **David Manuel** was the writer of more than fifty books, including the Faith Abbey Mystery series and such bestsellers as *The Light and the Glory* (coauthored with Peter Marshall). His most recent title, *Once Upon a Prayer,* is a little book on how to hear God in your heart. At the time of his death, David was working on *The Forge,* a novel of the winter of Valley Forge, when iron was refined into steel and a new nation's character was formed.

**Kathryn Ann Mays** is a visual artist, wife, mother of five, and guardian of Minnie the cat. Kathryn grew up on a dairy farm with many barn cats, and she has a soft spot for animals. Her favorite art projects are portraits of people or animals done in pencil, watercolor, and acrylic. You can learn more about Kathryn's art at www.kathrynmays.com.

**April McGowan**, her husband, two children, and her "mews," Spookers, live in the beautiful Pacific Northwest. When she's not writing, homeschooling her kids, or playing board games, you might find her at her drum kit, imagining she's on a world tour. To read other short stories, find out about her latest novel, *Jasmine*, and keep up with April in general, follow her blog at http://aprilmcgowan.com.

**Mark Muhich** currently writes a bi-monthly column about the environment for the Michigan newspaper *Jackson Citizen Patriot*. As chairman of the seven-county Central Michigan Group Sierra Club, many of his creative projects focus on conserving Michigan's natural beauty. His most recent artworks are realistic ceramic portraits of Michigan's eleven species of turtles, many of them threatened.

**Mary Ann Osborn** left Mississippi a few years after Hurricane Katrina and moved back to her home state of Michigan, where she spends lots of time with her ten grandchildren. She recently welcomed Percy, a white half-Maine coon, to her home in the country, followed by two parakeets, Romeo and Juliet. Percy yowls and the birds sing, so it's always lively in the house.

**Ed Peterson** still likes cats, but travel keeps him from having any right now. Ed is a third-generation "Yooper" (a native of Michigan's Upper Peninsula) who now lives in Michigan's Lower Peninsula with his wife, Christine, and son, Graham. Retired from forty years in education, Ed enjoys running, gardening, being active in his church, and working for social justice. Although

Ed's hair is shorter and thinner than it was in 1967, he says he's still living in the sixties inside.

**Dusty Rainbolt,** ACCBC, is editor-in-chief of AdoptAShelter .com (www.AdoptAShelter.com) and vice-president of the Cat Writers' Association (www.catwriters.org), as well as a member of the International Association of Animal Behavior Consultants, none of which would have been possible if she hadn't rescued Mom and her brood. Dusty is the author of *Cat Wrangling Made Easy: Maintaining Peace & Sanity in Your Multicat Home, Kittens for Dummies,* and several science fiction and fantasy novels. Her new novel is *Death under the Crescent Moon* (Yard Dog Press), and she edited and contributed to the recent anthology *The Mystical Cat.* Since Dusty began rescuing in 1996, she has rescued and re-homed over 1,200 cats and kittens.

**Ila J. Smith** grew up on a farm with many animals, including the traditional cats and dogs as pets, plus a short sojourn with a pet pig. She and her husband founded and owned a shopping guide/printing business for nearly twenty years. After she was widowed in her forties, she went on to become a city manager and a chamber of commerce executive, and she recently retired from leading a group in restoring the city's eighty-year-old historic theatre. Ila remained busy volunteering until her death three months before this book was published. Cindy Lou moved in with family members who adore her.

**Jill Eileen Smith** (www.jilleileensmith.com) is the author of *Sarai* and *Rebekah,* books one and two in the *Wives of the Patriarchs* series, and the bestselling *Wives of King David* series. When she isn't writing, she enjoys spending time with her family—in person or over the webcam—or hopping on a plane to fly across the country. She can often be found reading, testing new recipes, grabbing lunch with friends, or snuggling one or both of her adorable cats.

**Jeanette Thomason** is a freelance writer and book editor for WhiteStone Publishing. She leads WhiteStone Weekends in Colorado Springs, experiential workshops that combine walks in the wild with an exploration of how to bring the sense of place (spiritually and geographically) to writing. She's a former editorial director for WaterBrook, acquisitions editor for Revell, and women's magazine editor of *Aspire* and *Virtue*.

**Cathy E. Watkins** was born an Earnhardt and loves NASCAR racing. She is a wife, mother of two, and grandmother of four who has been married to her husband, Mike, for twenty-nine years. Cathy loves all animals and people, including strangers. She says, in fact, "I get along with 'strange' very well!" She has contributed writings to *The Dog Next Door* and to the cookbook *Pit Stop in a Southern Kitchen* by her mother, Martha Earnhardt, and Carol Bickford.

A wagging tail. A goofy, floppy-tongued smile.
An excited bark when your keys jingle in the door.

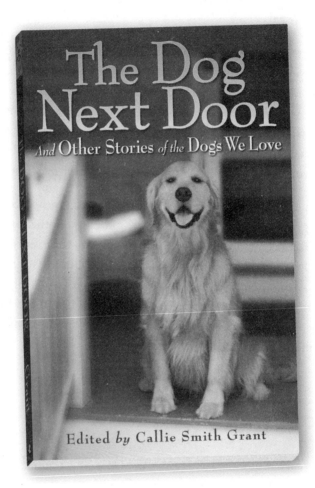

A heartwarming collection of true stories about the beautiful
relationship between people and their dogs.